38 YEARS

A DETROIT FIREFIGHTER'S STORY

Copyright © 2014 Bob Dombrowski
All rights reserved
First Edition

PAGE PUBLISHING, INC.
New York, NY

First originally published by Page Publishing, Inc. 2014

ISBN 978-1-62838-417-8 (pbk)
ISBN 978-1-62838-418-5 (digital)

Printed in the United States of America

The photographs in this book were provided by Bill Eisner and his book "We're Stretching" Mathew Lee and his book "Detroit Fire Department Apparatus History" The City of Detroit Photographers. Bob Johnson 3K Services. And my own personnel photographs.

This book is dedicated to the men and women both past and present, who served on the Detroit Fire Department. Detroit's bravest, America's best.

Acknowledgements

I'd like to thank my wife Linda for ever so patiently correcting my grammar, spelling, sentence structure, etc. Carolyn Walker, Kamie Crum, Mono D'angelo, Bill McGraw, and my three sons, Andy, Bobby, and Kevin, who each in their own way helped and encouraged me.

This is a story about my 38 years as a Detroit Firefighter. Everything I wrote about happened to the best of my memory. Some of the names I changed and some of the names I kept the same. I had to be careful because I still live in the Detroit area and they know where to find me.

CHAPTER 1

"Pans open," yelled the cook. I dropped the *Detroit Free Press* I was reading and headed back to the kitchen. There, half a dozen guys were herded around our big old Garland cast-iron stove with all its burners on. On top of each burner was a cast-iron frying pan with little chunks of fat burning to grease up the pan. In the center of the small kitchen was a square, green table piled high with food. Front and center were nine beautiful rib steaks (my favorite) sitting on the white wrapping paper they came in.

"Looks like the cook finally spent the money," somebody joked.

I grabbed the big fork, stabbed one of the steaks, plopped it in one of the sizzling pans, and sprinkled on salt and pepper and garlic powder. I grabbed a platter, scooped up a pile of mashed potatoes and some green beans, then stood around with everyone else, waiting for my rib eye to finish frying.

I finally headed, platter in hand, to the dining room, a long, narrow room adjacent to the kitchen. I found my seat at the heavy, oblong, fifteen-by-three-foot wooden table that was standard in every Detroit fire station. It could probably fit both units, about eighteen men, if you had to. I always sat on the side facing the windows. It was a pretty fall day with light gray skies. The leaves were changing, and a light wind was humming as I watched the cars quietly driving down West Grand Boulevard. I heard a dog bark behind me.

"Boze, I forgot about you," I said, laughing.

Boze was our fire station dog, a 150-pound half-shepherd, half-whatever-jumped-over-the-fence dog. She had wandered in one day a few years before and became part of our family. At the time, every fire station had a dog, and most fire-station dogs looked like Boze. Dalmatians are usually associated with firemen. Why? I don't know. I've never seen a Dalmatian in a fire station. Good old Boze sat there patiently as we feasted on our steaks, knowing afterward there would be her can of Kal Kan and a couple of bones, maybe even one with a little meat left on, for her.

Zing zing! The alert went off, as always, just as we started to eat. Our alert sounds like the bell you ring in a supermarket when you want the butcher. "Box alarm, everybody," yelled the man on watch. Oh boy! In Detroit we have three kinds of runs: box alarms, still alarms, and specials. Specials are runs that don't involve fire, such as car accidents, medical runs, people trapped in elevators, and so on. Still alarms are small fires, dumpsters, car fires, and the like. But box alarms are the big ones—building fires, house fires, store fires, and factory fires. And this was a box alarm, and when he shouted *everybody*, that meant everybody. We had two trucks, an engine and a ladder truck, and everybody was responding. We don't leave anyone at the fire station.

We all jumped up and ran to the apparatus room. There sat two well-worn fire trucks: Engine 10, a 1957 Seagrave fire engine, and Ladder 4, a 1958 Seagrave eighty-five-foot tiller ladder truck. A tiller ladder truck is a truck with a fireman who sits in the very back and steers the back end, and that was me.

I ran to the rear of the truck, jumped into my boots, threw on my coat, and climbed up into the bucket. I put on my helmet and hit the horn twice, two beeps, letting the driver know I was ready. Dino fired up the converted diesel, put it in gear, and out we went, lights flashing and sirens blaring. We went left and headed up to Michigan Avenue. When you're the tiller man and the driver turns left, you must turn right, keeping the back end in line.

In all my years as a firefighter, I've ridden and driven every type of fire apparatus imaginable, and I loved it all. But the most thrilling place to be is in the tiller bucket. Sure, you get wet when it rains and freeze in winter, but on this lovely fall afternoon, blasting down Michigan Avenue, this ride could have gone on forever. As we drove down this once-proud street lined with fading two-story buildings, some vacant, some with businesses still trying to hang on, there were a few pedestrians, most not bothering to lift their heads to look at this passing spectacle. After all, this is Detroit, fires and fire trucks are as common as robins in spring.

We made a sharp right on Twenty-Fifth, the engine first, closely followed by the truck. I could see the guys on the back of the engine, holding on with one hand as they strapped on their yellow MSA breathing tanks with the other. In Detroit, we pull up ready to fight fire.

We drove down Twenty-Fifth, a narrow street lined with small wood-framed houses built around the turn of the century. Most have been updated over the years from when Detroit was booming—asphalt siding in the thirties, aluminum siding in the fifties. Now these little houses sit like the rest of the city, trying to hold on, hoping for a better tomorrow. At the end of the street, like a castle in the middle of a village, was our destination, a huge cathedral-like church with smoke oozing out the roof overhangs. It was going!

The engine spun around and stopped in front of the church. The guys jumped off the back end, threw the two inch-and-a-half bundles down on the street, then grabbed the two-and-a-half-inch line, pulling off a couple of lengths, yelling "Okay." The FEO proceeded to the hydrant, jumped out, and began to hook up the soft suction to the fire hydrant. The ladder truck made a right turn to pull alongside the church while I maneuvered the back end between the fire engine and the parked cars. When Dino got the rig where he wanted it, he stopped, jumped out, and began putting out the outriggers.

The lieutenant yelled, "Put the stick up."

I knew what that meant. I climbed out of the bucket, unlocked the clamps that kept the tiller bucket in place, rolled the bucket over to free up the aerial ladder, reached down and pulled the pin up (the driveshaft that connects the steering wheel to the rear wheels), and threw it on the ground. The aerial was free, and Dino lifted it up and turned it to the top of the church roof. I ran to the toolbox, grabbed an axe, and waited, along with a firefighter I'll call Rodney, for the aerial to be in place so we could climb up and open the roof with holes.

Dino set the aerial in the center of the roof a couple of feet below the peak, which normally wouldn't be a problem. We climbed up the ladder, axes in hand, no air tanks, and no power saws. This was Detroit; we didn't have power saws back then. When we reached the peak, we went left, walking while straddling the peak. About twenty feet down, we stopped and began chopping a hole. The first thing we noticed was that this was a new roof. We rarely have fires with new roofs, and they are a lot harder to chop holes in. After a couple of minutes of chopping, we had a three-foot hole with a fair amount of smoke coming out. We decided to go to the other side of the aerial and put another hole in.

We went around twenty feet past the aerial and started chopping, but this time, it was different. Thick black smoke greeted us and some flames too. I looked back to our first hole. Thick black smoke was coming out of that one too, and the roof was getting hot. The smoke coming out of the eaves was getting thicker, and it was getting hard to see.

"We better get out of here," I said.

"You ain't kidding," said Rodney.

But now we had problems. The smoke was so thick we couldn't find the aerial, and it was getting hard to breathe. We crawled to where we thought the aerial was, but when we reached with our feet, we couldn't find it.

"It's got to be down here. I'm going to try," said Rodney.

"Man, be careful, because if you miss it, it's a long ride down, about forty feet," I said.

Slowly, he started to slide.

"It's not here," he yelled.

I reached down and helped pull him back up. It was getting darker and hotter and harder to breathe; time was running out. Nobody on the ground could see us. It was up to us. We slid a couple more feet down. This time, it was up to me. I handed Rodney my axe. Usually, you want it with you on a roof; punching the pick while slipping down a roof has saved many a fireman's life. This time, it wouldn't help. There was no time for a rescue. I started to freely slide down, kicking both feet, hoping to find the aerial. Suddenly, *bam*, my left foot hit it. I slid to it, grabbed on, and yelled, "Here it is." I kept yelling so Rodney could find me, and find me he did, sliding down dead center of the ladder. "Let's get the fuck out of here." And we did.

Back on the ground, we saw that the fire was starting to take control. It was coming through the roof. The engine crews were driven out of the church, and they were exchanging one-and-a-half-inch hose lines for bigger two-and-a-half-inch lines. The battalion chief called for a second alarm, which meant we would double the amount of men and fire companies we had on the scene.

Detroit's normal box-alarm response was three engines: one ladder truck, one squad, and a battalion chief, about twenty-two men in all. Calling for a second alarm would double that amount plus dispatch the senior chief to take charge. Each additional alarm after that, third, fourth, and fifth, would again dispatch that many companies and men to the scene. Fifth alarm is as big as they go in Detroit.

Ladder 4's crew was getting ready for the big show. The lieutenant ordered a water tower, which meant lowering the big aerial ladder down to its bed, installing a three-inch line with a big water gun (nozzle) on the very top. As we worked at that, the engine crew stretched two two-and-a-half-inch lines for our water supply. When ready, the driver cautiously raised the aerial ladder up while we installed the ladder straps and guide lines. This whole operation probably took three minutes while dodging smoke and debris from the fire.

Once the aerial was in place, towering over the church, a firefighter would have to go up and operate the water gun. I strapped on a safety belt and climbed up the big stick through all the smoke. When I reached the top, I knew something wasn't right.

The hose and the gun where shaking wildly. I couldn't see because of the smoke. I hooked in and reached over and turned the nozzle to fog to clear some of the smoke so I could see. What I saw was that the nozzle wasn't properly fastened and was about to fly off the aerial. The nozzle clamps to the first and second rung of the aerial. Our first rung was badly bent because we also use our aerial for ventilation. There was no better way to open up a dormer or a copula than with our power ram aerial ladder, but the years had taken their toll. The first rung was bent like a crescent and couldn't hold the nozzle clamp. To make matters worse, the spanner belt we used as a safety tie-down was left off during our haste in getting the tower up.

I grabbed on to both rungs using all my weight. I tried to keep the hose and gun in place. I began yelling down for them to shut the water off, but they were sixty feet below, and through the smoke, the sirens, the shouting, and the roaring fire, nobody could hear me.

Suddenly, the hose came off, flying right by me, pushing me off the ladder into the smoky sky. Luckily, the safety belt kept me from falling to the ground. The hose and gun went wild, like a loose giant cobra, showering the entire fire ground and everyone down there with hundreds of gallons of water. Boy, did they scramble! I pulled myself back on the aerial, unhooked my belt, and climbed down.

When I got to the bottom, the lieutenant asked, "You okay?"

"Yeah, I'm a little shook up, but I'm okay," I said.

We reassembled the water tower, properly this time. I went back up and began directing the water flow onto the burning church. I was suspended eighty-five feet in the air above the fire; I was like a bird, watching the whole operation. Below me, the fire was now coming completely through the roof; much of the roof was caving in. The fire had gone to a third alarm, and over a dozen trucks surrounded us. Two other aerial water towers were now operating, one in front and one in the rear. Fire hoses, looking like spaghetti, surrounded us. Firefighters on the ground operated monitors and two-and-a-half-inch lines, and together with our aerial attacks, the fire and the firefighters were at a standoff.

Looking down and to the left, I saw a half dozen Detroit cops standing around, looking sharp in their dark blue Eisenhower jackets. For them, it was momentarily soft duty, keeping the gawkers at bay, and they didn't seem to mind.

Past them, a crowd had gathered, as they always do. A lot of them looked elderly, old women in babushkas, old men in Andy Capp hats. I thought, what sacrifice they must have made working hard all day at the factories, coming home to those little houses, and building this church, which was now in flames. The church was something bigger than themselves, something they could all share, something they could all take pride in, something they all lived for, and now it was gone.

Looking farther, I could see the downtown skyline complete with our newest attraction, the Renaissance Center—five shiny cylinder skyscrapers built right on the Detroit River. The center was built by a group of civic leaders, including Henry Ford II, with the hope of turning around our dying downtown. They had a contest to name the center. I entered the name Emerald City from the movie *Wizard of Oz*. It kind of resembled it. After all, weren't all of us Detroiters as hopeful as Dorothy and the Tin Man were that this place would make everything all right? I didn't win. They chose the Renaissance Center.

After a few hours of us battling the blaze, the fire was starting to get under control. The chief called for relief, calling for replacement companies so we could go back to our quarters. Four hours is the longest they allow you to stay at a fire. The fire was still burning and would probably be for the rest of the night, meaning fire companies would be here all night. We were in a good spot, so the chief wanted our truck to stay as it was. We had no equipment to pick up. The relieving ladder company would simply replace us, and we would take their truck back to our quarters.

Our fill-in truck was a straight truck, no tiller, so I piled in back with everyone else. We all were cold, wet, exhausted, dirty, and hungry. I thought of my steak waiting for me. What would I do with it? Heat it up in the oven or maybe just get two slices of bread and make a steak sandwich. Decisions, decisions! When we got back, we found that the decision had already been made. My plate was empty. In fact, all the plates were empty, and scattered all about were nine steak bones licked clean. Lying in the corner was a guilty and overstuffed dog named Boze. Half the guys were yelling, and half were laughing. Poor Boze. After all, four hours is a long time to go without chow. I was so hungry I think I ate Boze's Kal Kan.

CHAPTER 2

1972

I was born and raised on the west side of Detroit. My father, like most of my friends' fathers, worked for the Big Three. I graduated from a Detroit public high school, got a job at Chrysler, and promptly got my ninety days in. I was all set, couldn't be fired now. I was in the United Automobile Workers.

My good buddy Gary Hogg worked alongside of me at Chrysler. Before that, we both worked together at a place called Built Right Modernization. In fact, just about every job I had was with Gary. Gary lived right down the street. We would always pick each other up for work. We both had red hair. Gary still wore his in a big pompadour, greaser style. Gary was well-known in the neighborhood as the best street racer; nobody could shift a four speed faster. That was a big thing in the sixties. Our rides to work, or school, were hair-raising. We would leave at the last minute then break every law on the books trying to get there on time. It was lots of fun.

We both lived with our folks. Gary's dad was a fireman, and unlike most dads in the neighborhood, Mr. Hogg was pretty cool. Back in the sixties, when everyone's folks drove station wagons or Buicks, Mr. Hogg drove a GTO. He had a pool in his backyard and, along with Mrs. Hogg, would be out there sunning, having a cocktail or two, right when I was picking Gary up for work. We were working afternoons.

"Gosh, it must be hot in that factory. You boys should get on the fire department," he said.

"I'd love to, Mr. Hogg," I'd say.

I went into the navy reserves. When I got back, I stopped over at Gary's.

"The fire department is giving out applications," he said. His dad had grabbed an extra one for me.

"What the heck," I said. I filled it out, and Gary's dad turned it in.

A couple of months later, I got a letter in the mail. It said that the following Saturday, I was to go take a test at Cobo Hall at 9:00 a.m. When I got there, it was packed. There must have been a couple thousand people there taking that test. It was like a high school reunion. Half of Cody, my high school, was there.

If you passed the written test, you were sent to the Detroit Fire Department Training Academy on the corner of West Warren and Lawton. There, we had to take an agility test. We had to climb a ladder, jump hurdles, and a bunch of other stuff, including climbing a rope without using your feet. I had never climbed a rope before, I told Gary, who was taking the test with me.

"It's easy. Just jump up high, grab the rope, and pull as fast as you can," he said.

I did and climbed all the way to the top. When I reached the top, I knew I was in, and nothing could stop me now. A few weeks after the tests, I received a card in the mail with the number 45 on it. That was where I placed among a couple thousand applicants. The card went on to say that when and if the city reached number 45, I would be called for the fire department. I put the card in my drawer and soon forgot about it. It would be a while before I would hear from the city.

I stopped by my parents' house one nice June Saturday for lunch.

"Hey, Bob, someone called you from the city, something about a fire department job, and for you to call her Monday morning," my mother said.

Wow, the fire department. I had forgotten all about it. It had been a couple of years, and my life and the world had changed so much. Still, I thought of Mr. Hogg lying by that pool.

My job at Chrysler had improved immensely. I was on the day shift, and they had made me an inspector. Not only that, but I soon would be getting an apprenticeship, the best thing you could get at an auto company. Doug Fraser, the president of the UAW, was a personal friend of my uncle and was helping me get one. But what was perfect was that I worked for Chrysler Export (back when America exported stuff). We would send car parts all over the world—Spain, Venezuela, you name it. When the orders came in, we worked ten- and twelve-hour days, plenty of overtime, and when there were no orders, we would get laid off for a few weeks or a month. We would load up a van and head to Florida, lying on a beach while collecting unemployment. Also, this was the early seventies, and we were all long-haired freaks, as we called ourselves. We hung out at the Grande Ballroom, east town theater, Dodge Park and The Florida Keys. I was having a blast. Did I want to give this up and join the straight life of a fireman?

Monday morning at my first break, I called the number my mother gave me. The lady from the city told me that they had *a position as a Detroit firefighter* for Robert Dombrowski starting next Monday. A position as a Detroit firefighter, the words moved around in my head. Nobody had ever used the word *position* and my name in the same sentence before. Positions meant you were somebody. Doctors had positions; lawyers had positions, pilots, dentists, teachers, cops, even carpenters, had positions. Factory workers didn't have positions. They were just workers. Yes, I wanted a position. She told me to report tomorrow morning at 8:00 a.m. to the city county building, and she gave me a room number.

The next morning, I called in sick at Chrysler, a not-so-easy thing because I was already on thin ice with my foreman for excessive absenteeism, and headed downtown to the city county building. I found the room, filled out a bunch of paperwork, and took a physical. After all that, they sent me to Detroit Fire Department Headquarters to take an additional physical. I needed directions.

Detroit Fire Department Headquarters was a four-block walk. When I got there, I found a five-story 1920s brick building sitting on the corner of Washington Boulevard and Larned Street. The first floor was around twenty feet high. Both the Washington Boulevard and the Larned side were lined with large, opened barn-type doors, and behind each door was a shiny red fire engine or a shiny red chief's car. The directory on the wall said that medical division was on the fourth floor. I took the rickety old elevator up to 4.

When I got off the elevator, there was a long hallway with open windows on the right and a row of glass-centered wood doors on the left. Under the row of windows were long wooden benches that were empty except for two individuals, who were both looking at me. I found the door that said Medical and went in.

Inside, there was an old wooden reception desk with an even-older-looking woman sitting behind it.

"Can I help you?" she asked.

"Yes, my name is Robert Dombrowski, and I'm here for my hiring physical," I said.

"I'm sorry, it's after eleven, and you will have to come back tomorrow," she said.

"What! Wait a minute. I was told to be at the city county building at eight, and I was. They sent me here. Please, you have to see me. I took the day off work, and I can't take another one tomorrow, can I?"

"You have to be here by eleven, and it's ten after. You want the job, you come back tomorrow."

"Damn," I said to myself.

When I stepped out of her office, the two guys sitting on the bench got up and approached me.

"We want to talk to you," one of them said. "If you want to be a firefighter, the first thing you have to learn is we have rules, and if you can't follow rules, you have no business coming on this job!" The other one just nodded his head approvingly.

"All right, I'll come back tomorrow."

Wednesday morning, I awoke and called off sick again. Boy, my foreman was really going to be angry. I headed downtown. After I passed my physical, they sent me down one floor to Operations. The first thing I noticed when I stepped off the elevator was a huge trophy case full of trophies that Detroit's firefighters' sports teams had won over the years. Across from the trophy case, hanging on the wall, were brass plaques awarded to Detroit from the US Chamber of Commerce for the best fire department in America. They were all from the thirties, forties, and fifties, back when Detroit was a rich city and spent accordingly. As I walked along the hall, I noticed how nice and quiet everything was. This must be where the big shots kept their offices. At the end of the hallway was a big room with an open door with a sign saying Operations hanging over the door.

I went in and laid the piece of paper Medical had given me on the counter. A captain got up, grabbed it, and handed me a stack of forms, some I had to sign, and some I kept. They told me when to report to the academy and what to wear—blue jeans and chambray shirts. Great! I had plenty of jeans. That's all I wore, plus I had a stack of chambray shirts courtesy of the US Navy. Last but not least, he handed me a sheet of paper called Directive 78, the haircut or grooming rule. The rule said you must have short hair cut above your ears and collar.

Now, this was 1972, and most of the captains and chiefs on the job were World War II vets, guys who flew in B-17s over Europe and hit the beaches in the South Pacific. They had crew cuts and wore white socks; they had military tattoos and smoked Luckies and Camels. This captain looked at me with a smile on the left side of his face while the right side clamped down on a burning Lucky.

"You got any problem with the haircut rule, kid?" he asked.

"No, sir," I lied.

When I got back down to the first floor, I walked around the apparatus floor, looking at the fire trucks. How understated they looked as they quietly rested. A bell rang, and someone yelled "Squad." A few men jogged over to a truck and climbed in the back; they were all clean-cut and wore dark blue uniforms. The fire truck started up, turned on its flashers, and pulled out onto Washington Boulevard. I followed them out and watched them maneuver through the downtown traffic. I watched until I couldn't see them anymore.

That night, we got the tribal council together. A half dozen of my friends and I sat around the room, drinking beers, listening to *Exile on Main St.* while discussing the biggest thing to happen to one of us in a while—me getting on the fire department—and what I should do.

"Man, that's a dangerous gig, running into burning buildings. No thanks," my friend Rich said.

Wally agreed and told us that when he was a kid, he was watching a big fire on Grand River and saw a fireman fall off an aerial ladder and land on the hood of the truck—a story I later checked out and found to be true.

Mark, always the pragmatic one, said, "Look, Bob, it's a steady job. Firemen never get laid off, and when you retire, you get a pension. How can you beat that?"

We went on all night, and the wisdom was rampant. In the end, I left early. I had to get up for work the next morning, and after missing two days this week, I couldn't be late. Besides, I knew what I would do, what I always do when I have to make a big decision: wait until the last moment.

Before I knew it, it was Friday, a half hour before quitting time, and I hadn't decided on anything. If I was going to be a fireman, I would have to go into the general foreman's office right now and resign from Chrysler. What was I to do? I couldn't decide. I was standing in front of the general foreman's office when a friend came running up, shouting, "Bob, we're getting laid off for two weeks." It's funny how life works; when you can't make up your mind, it makes it for you. So that's it. Tomorrow I get my locks cut off, and Monday, I show up at the Detroit Fire Department Academy, for two weeks anyway.

CHAPTER 3

On Monday morning, June 26, 1972, Gary and I drove to the DFD Training Academy for the first day of what would be our lifetime career. We parked in back and followed everyone into the rear door of this six-story brick building. The first thing we noticed was that there were no floors; we entered a huge brick training hall that was sixty feet tall. On the ceiling there were pulleys with ropes for firemen to slide down. Each floor had a balcony opening that was used for climbing and rappelling. Across the floor was a gabled, shingled roof that sat up about thirty feet. Ladders from twelve to fifty feet were neatly stacked up against a wall. A twenty-foot net was set up to catch someone falling. Next to the net was a fire hydrant opened so you could see the inner workings. On the wall behind it was a basketball hoop with Dillon 54 scrawled on it.

We were sent upstairs to a classroom. The walls were covered with pictures of firefighters performing various tasks over the years. Another wall had a wood board with various knots that we would have to learn. Throughout the room, we found firefighting tools and fittings that were either sitting on tables or hanging on walls. There was even a Gamewell telegraph system from the 1800s that the department was still using to send their runs.

One by one, we filed in. There were eighteen of us trial men, as they called us, to start. As I looked over my new class, I was very surprised to see a couple of people who I met before there. There, dressed in jeans and chambray shirts, were the two guys that gave me a hard time at Medical. Yes, these two jokers, who I shall refer to as Mutt and Jeff, were trial men, just like me. They both smiled and nodded sheepishly. I didn't return their greeting.

The instructors came in, and we all stood at attention. They introduced themselves as Lieutenant Watson, who looked like Dr. Watson in any Sherlock Holmes movie, and Lieutenant Blackmer, who looked like a character out of the TV show *77 Sunset Strip*. They told us what was expected of us these next four weeks. The training academy usually lasted eight weeks, but because of the large amount of firefighters that the city had hired, three hundred, the largest amount ever, our class time would be cut in half. We would still have to learn everything that an eight-week class would learn. We had to maintain an 85 percent average on all our tests. If we were late or absent, we would be taken down on charges. *Charges* was the term that the fire department called their discipline hearings. One good thing they said was that we were all getting a raise. Our starting salary was $7,800 a year, but because of a new union contract, it would go up to $8,200. First day on the job and I got a $400 raise. I must have been doing pretty well, I thought.

Our second day, we hit it pretty hard. As usual, with most military-type organizations, you start with marching. We were all out on the parking lot, marching back and forth, doing "dress right, dress" and all that stuff, when it became apparent that half our class hadn't been in the military and didn't know how to march. So the instructors divided us in half. The ones who didn't know how to march would stay here and practice, leaving a trial man we called Question, who seemed to be the best marcher, in charge. Lieutenant Watson took the rest of us to the classroom to begin our lessons.

A few hours later, a firefighter came running in and said, "There's a group of trial men down there that have been marching for over three hours, and one of them just fell out!"

"Okay, let's all take a break," Lieutenant Watson said.

We weren't the only class in the academy. Another class was there, and they were in their last week and would graduate Friday. The reason for the double classes, we were told, was that the city placed us in the year's budget that expired July 1. Had they not gotten our two classes in May and June, we would never have been hired.

We spent our lunch hour eating while watching the senior class with amazement. Everything they did was fifty feet in the air, sliding ropes and climbing ladders.

"This is crazy," I said to Gary. "In two weeks, I'm going back to Chrysler. You can get killed doing this stuff!"

"Not me, I'm staying," replied Gary, while straining his head to watch.

But soon, they had us doing the same crazy stuff. They start you off low, the second floor, then the third, then next thing you know, your five floors up, hanging out of a balcony window. They partner you up for all your aerial drills. My partner was an east-sider, also named Bob, who had just returned from Vietnam. Either out of wisdom or humor, the instructors put Mutt and Jeff together as partners. They were both afraid of heights! Not that any of us were 100 percent comfortable up there, but we managed a little better.

A favorite climbing exercise we did was the pompiers. Pompier ladders or hook ladders, from the term *hook and ladder*, are eight-foot-long wood poles with a hook on the top that you can hook on a windowsill. You and your partner climb to the top floor and back down using them. The whole class would be finished and sat and watched Mutt and Jeff, who would just be on the second or third floor going up, arguing all the way.

"You don't have it hooked in," yelled Mutt.

"No, no, it's hooked in," responded a shaken Jeff.

We would climb a forty-foot ladder held straight up by six men with ropes in what we called the church raise. When you got to the top of the ladder, you and your partner would switch sides and climb down. We would then climb to the top floor of the drill hall, go to the balcony, hook belts with our partners, put our hands behind our backs and hang out at a forty-five-degree angle fifty feet in the air. We slid down on the ropes and free-fall five stories, and we also used the ropes to rappel five stories.

We had another exercise. They would extend a thirty-foot straight-beam ladder between a balcony and the gabled roof about thirty feet off the ground. You had to walk from the balcony to the peak and back. Men walked and kids crawled, the instructors said. I figured there's no harm in being a kid, but the guy who went in front of me, a little wiry guy, did a dance going across it. The instructors roared with approval. Now it was my turn. What could I do? I couldn't crawl now. I did my slowest granny walk, no dance steps. I'll save them for later.

Learning to tie all the knots was very stressful. Knot-tying was taught by Lieutenant Blackmer, who had very little patience. "I'm going to show you guys how to tie a becket bend, so pay attention," he would say. He would then grab two ropes, tying them very fast, then he would hand you the two ropes and expect you to be able to tie them just like he did. I grabbed the ropes and fumbled around the best I could. He then grabbed them back, yelling at me for not paying attention. Back and forth, this would go on for days, you fumbling, him screaming, until surprisingly, you learned the knots.

The hardest event, we all agreed, was the smokehouse. A twenty-by-ten-foot wood shed with a pointed roof and no windows. It had a potbellied stove next to it with its exhaust pipe going into the shed. They would make a wood fire in the stove, and it would fill the smokehouse with thick black smoke. It's no longer used; it was closed years ago by the EPA and various human rights groups. But for us, it was there, and right after lunch, we had to go through it. "Don't eat too much at lunch," they humorously warned us.

It was simple enough they said. We went in the front door and came out the back door, except the interior was a cut-up maze that we had to find our way through. We crawled left, right, up, and down, all in pitch-black smoke with no air to breathe. We weren't allowed to wear our air masks. We were taught that in fires, there was a little oxygen to breathe just above the floor. It was 1972, and Detroit firefighters believed you had to be able to take the smoke to survive fires.

The first one through was Mark Bigly. He was fairly brave and first on a lot of things. When he finally got through, he had snot down to his knees. "It's a motherfucker in there," he cried. I was second. I took a deep breath and went in, crawling on my hands and knees, following their instructions, "Go left, go right, go up, go down." A couple of times I crawled back down to the floor just to get a breath of air.

You couldn't see or breathe. I finally came to the door, opened it, and jumped out. Snot was down past my knees. Yes, I made it!

One by one, the rest of the class went through. They had two emergency trapdoors on top in case someone panicked, but they didn't have to open them for us. We all made it. Mutt and Jeff were the last to go. It took Jeff a couple of tries before he got through. Mutt made it through the first time, but he threw up all over the place. Must have been something he ate.

The city was in the process of hiring an additional three hundred firefighters, and they were bringing them in every afternoon to take their agility test. This became our new lunchtime entertainment. We would finish eating then climb up on the net and watch, laugh, taunt, and cheer, with the white guys cheering for the white guys and the blacks cheering for the blacks. Afterward, we would kid each other who was best at climbing the ropes, jumping the hurdles, and climbing the ladders. I recognized a few guys from my old neighborhood and wished them luck.

On the second-to-the-last day, we were given our accumulated test score. Three guys who didn't maintain an 85 percent were let go. One of the people let go was no surprise. He had a full-time job working the night shift at Chrysler and used his academy time to catch up on his sleep. But it was sad to see the other two go. Then they loaded us up on a couple of old fire trucks and drove us to DFD apparatus for all our new gear. We were given two sets of dark blue Sanforized work uniforms. We were allotted six, and we would get the other four when we completed our probationary period. Then we were given three quarter-length boots, a rubber fire coat, a pair of thin yellow gloves that everyone threw out, a breathing mask, and a helmet, which they ran out of, telling us to borrow one until they got some more.

My phone rang as I was sitting at home that last night; it was Gary.

"Bob, the transfer list is out. Do you want to know where you're going?"

"What difference does it make? There are fifty fire stations. The only one I know is Engine 55, Joy Road, and Southfield. That's the one that's by my house, and I'm probably not going there," I said.

"No, you're not going there, but you'll know this one. We all know this one. You're going to Engine 12," he laughingly said.

Oh no, anything but Engine 12, I thought. Engine 12 is the fire company that runs out of the front of the academy. I wouldn't be going anywhere. All my classmates would be leaving the academy tomorrow, going to such exotic places as Grand River and Meyers or East Jefferson and Copeland, and I'd be stuck right there with the instructors breathing down my neck. What did I do to deserve this?

The next day was graduation. We scrubbed the drill hall and set up the podium and the chairs. The mayor and the chief of department were coming. Our families were coming. We had our new uniforms on. We would slide ropes and climb ladders and show the world all the new stuff we had learned.

To my surprise, a few of the girls from my crowd showed up. How they knew about my graduation, I didn't know. But they looked great, nice dresses, hair and makeup to the nines. Also, in the crowd looking at me mockingly was my new crew from Engine 12.

They called us up one by one to get our graduation certificates. I was the last one called, and when they called my name, all my girlfriends stood and cheered at the top of their lungs! I saw the Engine 12 crew, the guys I would be running with in a couple of days, and they were now looking at me approvingly. What a difference a few pretty faces make.

After Graduation the whole class went to some eastside bar called the Red Balloon. Mutt and Jeff picked it out. We were surprised when the waitress informed us that Jeff, a steady customer, was a fire lieutenant. Here we thought he was just a trial man like us. We had a wonderful time, drinking beer and reminiscing. When it came time to divvy up the tab, we tried to get Jeff to kick in a little extra. We said, "Hey, aren't you a lieutenant?" Jeff just paid the same as us. Leaving, we bid our farewells and good-lucks, knowing that on Monday, we would all be at our new fire stations, listening to the radio and the tape, waiting for our first fire. Who would be the first one of us to get a fire? We all hoped to be the one.

CHAPTER 4

Monday morning at 0700 hours, I walked in the back door of Engine 12 dressed in my new Sanforized uniform, carrying all my fire gear. The first person I encountered was a firefighter, who looked like he had been up all night, leaning on the kitchen counter, reading the morning paper while sipping on his coffee. He turned his head in my direction and said, "Throw your gear on the back of the rig, kid, then go find the lieutenant." He then returned to his paper.

I dragged my gear into the apparatus room, and there it was, Engine 12. Engine 12 was a new fire engine, a red Mack 1000 GPM pumper. At the time, Detroit had two types of fire engines, the new Macks and the older Seagraves. The Macks, unlike the Seagraves, carried a two-hundred-gallon water tank with a high pressure one-inch red line. This meant that at small fires, cars and trash fires, you would just pull off the red line and use the tank water to put the fire out. Afterward, you just pushed a button and the line rolled back up. The Seagraves had no water tank. With the Seagraves, you always used the heavy inch-and-a-half line and then stretched another line to the hydrant for your water, a much harder task.

I went to the right side of the rig behind the officer's seat, as I was taught. I removed the firefighter's gear that I was relieving, placed my boots on the ground, ready to jump into them. I pulled off the MSA air pack, checked it, making sure there was two thousand PSI on the gauge, and then I attached my facepiece. I laid out my fire coat and gloves on the seat in a way that would be easy to put on. I didn't have a helmet, something I would have to tell the lieutenant.

The officers' rooms and the watch room were located in the front of the station. A group of guys were sitting around the watch desk. I entered, and off they went. "What the heck is this? Don't tell me you're our new trial man. Couldn't they send us anything better?" And on and on the jokes came. Standing in the center of this group, not saying anything, only looking with a practiced look of confusion on his face, was Lieutenant Paul.

"Good morning, sir," I said as I saluted.

"And a good morning to you, Trial Man Dombrowski. Welcome to Engine 12," Lieutenant Paul responded with a little laughter from the men.

Lieutenant Paul found me a fire helmet and then spent the next two hours going over every inch of the rig. He was a wiry guy, about forty-five, a World War II vet who wore his graying hair in a crew cut and usually had a lit Winston on his fingers. He had a wry sense of humor, and it didn't take long to figure out that he was a fireman's fireman, well respected by his crew. He ran a tight ship.

When Lieutenant Paul finished, he assigned another firefighter to show me the housework. Trial firefighters were expected to work nonstop from seven in the morning until eight at night, mopping floors, washing windows, washing walls, and cleaning attics. Always have a rag in your pocket and never stop moving, as the saying goes.

I was upstairs in the dorm room. A firefighter named Sam was showing me how to make the beds when the alert went off.

"Is that the alert?" I asked.

"Yeah, it's the alert. Let's go!" Sam said.

We slid down the pole, and I ran to the rig as I heard someone yell out "Engine." I jumped into my boots and put the rest of my gear on, just as Lieutenant Paul told me to. He came running around the front of the rig, looked back as he was climbing in, and said, "Don't fall off."

We pulled out of quarters, made a left, and headed west on Warren Avenue, lights flashing and sirens blaring. It was a surreal moment every firefighter experiences on his first run. I was thinking that I am now a firefighter, a person who will come when there is trouble and whatever that trouble is, I would have to be able to take care of it. Wow, what a responsibility! That's why we have fire departments, and screaming down the road was the fire department with me being part of it. It was crazy.

We went a while down Warren Avenue then made a right turn on a side street and came to a quick stop in front of a house. Behind the house, smoke was coming out of the garage. Lieutenant Paul ordered me to stretch the red line. I grabbed the red line and pulled it to the garage. Inside, there was a small pile of trash burning, and we quickly extinguished it. Then we dragged the line back to the rig. Out front, the lieutenant was joking around with some civilians as he was writing down information. We all piled back on the rig, and as quick as we came, we were gone.

That would be the only run I would have on my first day. I spent the rest of my first shift cleaning and standing watch. Evening chow was rib steaks; it was the first time I had ever had one. It was Lieutenant Paul's first day as a lieutenant, and he paid for the steaks.

Unfortunately, I found out that this would be the only day I would be working with Lieutenant Paul and the rest of his crew. That day, I would only work twelve hours, half a day, and I would have to come back tomorrow and work on the other unit, unit 2. The fire department is divided into two units, and your unit is always the good unit, and the other unit is always the bad unit. As I left for home, they bid me farewell and wished me luck with the bad unit. I hoped in this case it wasn't true.

Tuesday morning, at 0700 hours, I came through the back door; it was my second day on the job and with a new unit. The first thing I noticed was that the men on this unit were a little younger and a little looser than those on unit 1. A couple of the guys were in the kitchen, and they asked me if I knew the routine, if I'd had a fire yet, and who the girls were that came to my graduation. Then they sent me up front to meet my new captain. Captain Adams asked me the same questions the guys in the kitchen asked, except about the girls at graduation. He then asked if I was married and if I was a hunter. I said no to both.

"Too bad," he said, "hunters have sons, and non-hunters have daughters." A prediction I would later prove wrong. He then called over Ken, the last trial man, to show me what I had to do every day.

Ken loved this; he had been the youngest man here for the last year and a half. Now he had somebody below him, someone else to do the nasty work. And nasty it was. He started with the bathrooms that had to be scrubbed and cleaned every day. The next stop was the dorms. I had to dust-mop and make the beds each morning. The apparatus floor was hosed and mopped every morning, but everyone usually pitched in for that. The stoves and refrigerators were wiped down every day and scrubbed once a week. Windows were done on Mondays, and brass, including the two brass poles, would be polished every Saturday. The list went on and on, and when I wasn't working, I had to stand watch. I was also responsible for the journals and the run books.

Standing watch meant that I sat at the watch desk, listening to the radio and watching the tape for fire calls that your station responded to. A fireman always had to be at the watch desk. Missing a run is a serious offense. The watch desk was also where they kept the journals and run books.

Ken then told me the two most important rules for a trial man. The first rule—always be busy. Whenever the captain sees you, make sure you're doing some work. And the second, and by far the most important—at fires, make sure that you have the pipe (hose nozzle). Never ever give up the pipe! The person on the pipe is the first one in. He is the one taking the most heat. He is the one putting out the fire. And it better be you. On this job, your reputation is everything, and if you don't follow those two rules, you will never make it.

A few hours later, when I finished cleaning, I was sitting at the watch desk, reading the rule book, just like we were supposed to, and a fireman named Ralph came in and asked, "Aren't you the new trial man?"

Ralph was our cook. Firemen work a twenty-four-hour shift, so we ate at the station. One person was assigned as cook. We gave him our chow money. Three dollars a day was the charge when I started in 1972. It would be fifteen dollars a day when I retired thirty-eight years later. He then was allowed to leave quarters for a couple of hours to shop for food. When he returned, he would spend most of his day in the kitchen, cooking. We would have two meals, one at noon and the other at six. At least that was when we were supposed to eat. We usually ate a little later.

"Yes, sir, I am the new trial man," I respectfully replied.

"Well, put that stupid rule book down and follow me to the kitchen," he said.

"Listen," Ralph told me, "the best job for a trial man is helping the cook. If you sit at the watch desk, the bosses will always find a bunch of bullshit for you to do. So in the morning, get your work done, then when I get back from shopping, meet me in the kitchen, and you'll be the cook's helper."

"Sounds good to me," I said.

And good it was. Nobody can cook better than a fireman, and Ralph was a great cook. I learned how to peel potatoes and how to make a great piecrust. Everything we made, we made from scratch, no Betty Crocker mixes here. We made beef stroganoff, Swiss steak, pasta sauces, soups, pies. We even made our own noodles with flour, water, and a rolling pin. Also, the kitchen was where all the socializing took place, and being the cook's helper, I would be right in the middle.

But you're not really a firefighter until you get a real fire. It was my third day, and I still hadn't had a working fire, a good building fire. I was keeping track of my classmates, and most had had working fires. Some had already been to more than one. Engine 12 was a top-ten company for fires, but I began to wonder. I was even ribbing the guys about how slow we were.

I was just finishing the evening dishes when the alert went off.

"Engine, box alarm," someone yelled.

I dropped my towel and ran for the rig. As I was snapping up my fire coat, Ralph ran up and said, "I guarantee you have a fire."

We pulled out of quarters heading east. The fact that the truck, Ladder 9, which ran out of our quarters, wasn't coming with us, meant that the run was not in our first alarm district, and we would be the second or third engine on the scene. I would have a couple of extra minutes to get ready. As we got closer, I could smell wood burning, like I was up north at a campfire. But we weren't up north; we were in the hood. Ralph was right; we got a fire.

We pulled up to a three-story apartment building. There were fire trucks everywhere and firemen in black fire coats and black helmets, pulling hoses and putting up ladders and yelling orders. I looked up and could see smoke coming out of the second- and third-story windows. I jumped off the rig and ran for the front entrance. I was scared shitless. Inside, there was a stairway going up with two hose lines stretched up and a lieutenant at the top of the stairs, kneeling down, trying to escape the smoke. Officers rarely wore air tanks back then; they must have had lungs made of leather.

Behind me, someone yelled, "Squad, let's go!" The firemen assigned to squad trucks were also paramedics. The first engine crew found an unconscious woman on the third floor, and the squad had to rush her to the hospital. Squads did most of the medical runs back then. The squad guys were the ones on the hose line, and they had to drop it and go. The lieutenant on the top of the stairs turned to me and said, "You put your mask on and get up there and man that line."

I pulled my mask over my face and reached back and turned my tank on. I went up the stairs and turned right to follow the line. I couldn't see anything because of the smoke. It was all black. I was a blind man in a hostile world. It was terrifying! I crawled along the hose line, all alone, not knowing where I was. I didn't know where Tim, the guy riding with me, was. Two firefighters passed by me in the blackness, going the other way. Must be the squad crew, I thought. "The pipe is a few feet down," they told me. I followed the hose line until I found the hose nozzle, the brass Rockwood pipe that we used back then, and began dragging it down the hallway toward were I thought the fire was. Suddenly, Tim showed up.

"Is that you?" he shouted through his mask.

He found the apartment door and shouted, "When I pop this door, you be ready with the water."

He popped opened the apartment door, and the heat shot out like a blast furnace. I pulled back on the Rockwood handle and began shooting water straight into the apartment and on the ceiling above to cool us off. Tim stayed right behind me, directing my every movement. We slowly crawled forward. I was squirting water in every direction except behind us. Through the thick black smoke, I could see a reddish glow. That's what fire looks like to firemen in burning buildings, not the flames you see in the movies, and I saturated that glow with 120 gallons of water a minute. Inside the burning room, all the loud noises you hear outside cease except for dull thuds, like if you were punching the walls. That's the sound the squirting water makes.

The truck crews, using twelve-foot-long pike poles, wood poles with metal hooks on the tips, smashed the exterior windows. It seemed like they turned on a huge exhaust fan as the temperature dropped by a hundred degrees. Black smoke poured out the windows as the smoke lightened up inside. We moved from the living room to the kitchen then the bedroom, knocking down the fire. More firemen came in with axes and six-foot pike poles and began ripping the walls and ceiling apart and throwing burning stuffed furniture out the windows. Look out below!

Once the fire was knocked down, I pulled my face piece off, even though the place was still full of smoke, and then went to the window, turned the pipe to fog, and fogged the place out. The guys asked if I needed a break; the answer was no! I kept the pipe until they shut the water off at the fire engine. I then dragged it outside, disconnected it, and helped load the line back on the rig. Never give up the pipe.

Backing into quarters was cool. Ralph was waiting, and I told him he was right. We'd had a fire. I was totally exhausted, filthy dirty, and soaking wet. I was proud of myself. My first real fire and I got the line. I went to the slop sink and scrubbed off, cleaned my facepiece, and filled my air tank up. I then got a cold pop out of the machine and wondered when my next fire would be. I didn't have to wonder long. Three hours later, we had another one.

CHAPTER 5

Wayne State University is a huge college complex that is in an area of Detroit called Midtown. Back in 1972, WSU was buying property to expand their campus. Expansions in Detroit follow a usual pattern. First, they make a proposal to tear down a neighborhood to build something new. Second, the residents protest until the city offers them more than their houses are worth. Third, the residents move out, leaving the area vacant. Forth come the fires, and do they come.

It was a beautiful old neighborhood filled with Victorian-styled houses. The homes had fallen under disrepair, and most were vacant. One night, we stretched on a house on a street called Commonwealth. The next morning, the paper had an article headlined Charles Lindbergh's Boyhood Home Burns. Turns out that Lindbergh grew up in Detroit. His mother was a Detroit schoolteacher, and that was their house that burned down last night. Who knew?

We were second engine to the area, and we were getting good fires there every night. Engine 5 was first engine. At the time, they were the busiest engine in the city. A fireman a few years older than me who used to hang out at the gas station I worked at in high school was assigned to Engine 5. Back then, everybody called him Fireman Freddy, but now, he went by the name of Wolfman. That's the name he had on the back of his coat.

We pulled up second engine. We had a big old Victorian house burning throughout, and there, up on a porch overhang, was the Wolfman. He was by himself on an inch-and-a-half line, knocking down fire through a window, and was getting ready to enter. My captain told me to back him up, and I gladly climbed up onto the overhang. The roof was wet, and Freddy backed up, and I slipped off the roof, falling to the ground.

Freddy climbed down to see if I was all right. I was more embarrassed than anything else. But my right hand was bloody; the axe I was holding had somehow cut my right ring finger when I fell. I would need stitches.

"Well, kid, welcome to the fire department. You will get a lot more injuries worse than that," Freddy said.

"Thanks, Freddy," I told him.

This would be the first of many injuries. The squad transported me to Detroit Receiving Hospital. Detroit Receiving was an old limestone building in the heart of the city, the place where indigents and people without insurance are transported to. Cops would walk around with handcuffs with long chains on them. The hallways were filled with injured victims chained to their gurneys, yelling, screaming, and cussing anybody who walked by. Doctors who'd seen it all treated them with indifference.

Being an injured firefighter, you're treated differently than the general public. They attend to you right away, no wait, as opposed to all those suffering patients in the hallway. The doctors and nurses were very nice and had my finger stitched in a few minutes.

The nurse was bandaging my finger when I heard a voice say "If you two are done holding hands, maybe I can take you back to your quarters." It was the senior chief, and he didn't seem very happy to be here at four in the morning. I climbed into the back of his big red Chrysler. Back then, the senior chief had his own driver. They drove me back to quarters. As I was getting out of his Chrysler, I asked if I could go home. "No," he said, "you remain on duty. Don't ride the rig for the rest of the night, and tomorrow, be at medical division at 0800 hours."

The next morning, I reported to the medical division. I found an empty spot on an old wooden bench by all the other injured firefighters. There must have been twenty of us, and the number was growing. I sat there for three hours before they called my name. They placed me on light duty until I got my stitches out. This meant that I could do everything except ride the rig. Now this would cause a problem. As a trial firefighter, you kept track of all your fire service. Our class was competing for who got the most fire service. I knew a couple of days of not riding the rig would hurt my numbers; I was already behind Gary Hogg at Engine 49.

Each day, I grew a little more into this strange new world called the Detroit Fire Department. I learned more of their traits and customs, their friendship and their camaraderie. At the time, there were 1,800 Detroit Firefighters, mostly white and all males. It was more like a club than a job, a brotherhood where everybody helped and pulled for each other. We risked our lives together, worked together, and socialized together.

Part of the socializing happened each morning after the cook got back from shopping. The guys would assemble in the kitchen and have a few cold beers. Sure, it was against the rules, but this was 1972, when businessmen enjoyed three martini lunches, and drinking a few beers was an accepted part of our culture. Firefighters thought it made them better firefighters. It took away some of your fears and inhibitions. Drinking beer helped you to inhale smoke; we seldom wore air tanks back then.

Who could eat, or take, the most smoke was a big deal to Detroit firefighters back in the old days. Air tanks were for pussies; we only used them when we absolutely had too. It was quite common to see firefighters out front of a burning building throwing their guts out or getting oxygen. The old pros used to reach down and turn the new guys' air tanks off right in the middle of a burning building. You couldn't breathe, then you would panic until you realized what happened. I have even seen two firemen make a bet then go out back and light a dumpster on fire to see who could hold their heads in there the longest.

The Detroit Fire Department started in 1867, two years after the Civil War. Back then, firemen had to work six twenty-four-hour shifts a week with only one day off a week. They had no kitchens at the firehouses. Firemen were allowed to go home twice a day, at noon and again at 6:00 p.m., for their meals. A fireman's nickname for children way back then was mealers. You can guess where that name came from. A little more was going on than just eating their meal.

Twice a day, every morning and every evening, a horse-drawn cart would come by and bring bottles of hot coffee. And to fill in the gaps, the local saloons would deliver buckets of beer. The tradition would continue for a hundred years, right up to the 1970s. The buckets of beer were replaced by cases of cans—boxes, we called them—of Altes beer delivered right to the fire station by Altes beer trucks.

Altes was the beer of choice for Detroit's bravest. For $3.50 a case, how could you go wrong? Any fire station that was drinking beer would be drinking Altes. At home, on vacation, you name it, that's what we drank. The firemen bars that we frequented all had Altes on tap. Altes was brewed in Detroit on Mack Avenue, so we were helping out a taxpayer.

We drank our beer in empty green-pea cans or yellow-corn cans or in whatever vegetable cans that the cook brought back. Although drinking was common, it was against the rules. So to hide it from the captain or the chief, we would drink out of the pea cans. If a chief came into the kitchen, we just placed the cans on the cupboard shelf. Nobody could tell what we were doing. To this day, when I'm cooking at home and using a can of something, I empty it and fill it with beer. It's still the best beer mug in the world.

Firemen were tough guys who could handle the toughest situations and who deserved a couple of cold beers. There weren't fights or accidents or mishaps at fires, just some good-natured socializing. Those days are sadly gone and will never come back.

I was reminded of them a few years back. The department sent me to Eastern Michigan University for staff-and-command school. We had a class in health. The professor said, "If you take two individuals, same age, same size, and the same eating habits, the only difference is one drinks two to three alcohol drinks a day and the other one doesn't drink. You will find that the drinker will live, on average, three years longer than the nondrinker."

If it is true that a nondrinker lives less than a drinker, then it is also true that a non-firefighter lives longer than a firefighter. According to the experts, firefighters have a ten-year-shorter life expectancy because of all the smoke, chemicals, and dangers they face. So firefighters should enjoy a few drinks daily. Losing seven years of your life is better than ten. Where the heck is my pea can?

Drinking wasn't the only activity we did in our off time. Ping-Pong, pool, basketball, working out, fixing cars, fixing the fire station, you name it, firemen did it. Best of all were the pranks. When you bought a new car, through pranks, you would be convinced that you bought a lemon. If you picked the wrong spot to sit, you got drenched by a bucket of water. They short-sheeted your bed, put water in your boots, put hot sauce in your food, and on and on, but the best prank of all was Moe.

Moe was the prank that the guys pulled on every new trial man, and it was a beauty. The story went like this. Moe's whole family was killed in a fire a few years ago. Moe was the only one to escape. He was badly burned, including his face, and he lost a leg. For all this, he blamed the fire department and wanted revenge. One night, he broke into a fire station and attacked the man on midnight cot watch with a knife. He was arrested and thrown in jail. And guess what, he just got out, vowing more vengeance to the fire department.

Now nobody in their right mind, especially a trial man who's been the brunt of numerous pranks, would believe this story, not at first. But the story went on for days and then for weeks, even months. They methodically built it up. Everyone was in on it. "Moe tried to get into Engine 10 last night! Moe tried to bust into Engine 31! The cops almost caught him!" The Moe stories went on and on until you started to believe them. Then it was my turn to stand my first cot watch.

Cot watch is the watch where one person sleeps downstairs by himself. He mans the watch desk from midnight to six thirty in the morning. He is responsible for all the calls his station receives. I was nervous enough thinking that I might be sleeping and miss a run, and now I had this Moe nonsense that I half-believed to worry about.

The evening started out with the police pulling up to quarters with their flashers on, telling me that they had Moe surrounded just down the street. An hour later, they came back and said that somehow Moe got away, so be sure to lock the doors tonight. So there I was, lying on the cot, waiting for the inevitable. About 1:00 a.m., it started—thump slide, thump slide—the unmistakable sound of a crippled person walking in my direction. Suddenly, there he was, knife in hand

and some weird mask on his face. I yelled, "Moe's here," but nobody came down. Moe ran away, and I sat there thinking, how dumb was I to believe this crap?

The next morning, I could tell the guys weren't quitting. "So Moe came and he almost got you?" they asked. I went along with them, trying to think of a way I could turn the prank around on them.

My next day at work, I was ready for Moe. I had a little starter pistol in my pocket, the kind they used at track events, the kind that shoots blanks. All day long, it was Moe this and Moe that, and I went along with them. That night, for some reason, I had to stand cot watch again. As I lay there, waiting, I was laughing so hard I was almost crying. Then I heard it, the familiar thump-slide sound. I silently waited. Then there he was, knife in hand and that same ridiculous mask on his face. I jumped off the cot, pulled out my pistol, and shot him a couple of times as I yelled, "I got him. I shot Moe!" Poor Bob Collins, who played Moe, had dropped his knife and was looking at his chest for bullet wounds.

"You asshole," he screamed. "You scared the shit out of me. I thought you shot me!"

This time, everybody came running down, thinking I shot Bob Collins. I was laughing so hard that they started laughing too. Even the captain thought it was funny and wasn't mad that I woke him up. Years later, the story grew to the gun being real. I just went along with it and said, "Lucky I'm a bad shot."

CHAPTER 6

After six months as a trial firefighter, I was confirmed as a firefighter. The department presented me with a badge; my new badge number was 842, which became my favorite number. Now I was a firefighter, not a trial man. I got to take naps in the afternoon, take details to other fire stations, and I could join in the engine house activities and become one of the boys. Also, at six months, you usually got transferred from an engine company to a truck company.

No problem, I thought. They would transfer me across the floor, from Engine 12 to Ladder 9. I loved running here, and my crew was a lot of fun. We were a busy fire station, top 10 in the city and a double house with ten guys on duty, so there was always something going on.

But the department had other plans for me. Unlike every member of my class who was transferred across the floor, I was transferred to another fire station, Ladder 22. Why this happened to me, I wasn't sure. Was it because someone at Ladder 22 wanted me or someone at Engine 12 didn't want me? What difference did it make? I packed up my gear at Engine 12, bid the guys a sad farewell, and headed to my new home.

There are two types of firefighters, one who starts at one place and then spends practically his entire career there, and type two, guys who make every transfer list. I didn't know it at the time, but I was type two. Every six months, the department put out a transfer list, and every six months, my name would be on it. After a while, it became second nature, a new place, new people, and a new district to learn. There were ninety fire companies in Detroit back then, and between transfers and details, I spent a twenty-four-hour tour at every one of them. Engines, trucks, squads, the snorkel, the boat tender, even the department ambulance, I hit them all. But my first new stop would be Ladder 22.

Ladder 22 was a sleepy single-company fire station located in an old Polish neighborhood. It was only three miles from Engine 12, but it was worlds apart. Engine 12 was a busy double house; ladder 22 was a slow single house. Engine 12 had two new modern rigs; ladder 22 had one sixty-five-foot Seagrave service truck that was over twenty years old and looked every bit of it. And as old as the truck was, it was still the youngest thing there. The crew was made up of a bunch of firefighters with over twenty years of seniority, waiting to be promoted to sergeant. The fact that I had my firefighter's badge meant nothing to this crew. As far as they were concerned, I was still a brand-new trial man.

But it was still a great job and one that I was glad to have. After a while, I started to get used to my new quarters. As the young guy, I was expected to take all the details, do all the dirty jobs, and stand the cot watches. I couldn't blame the crew. They all had enough time where they should be officers by now, so why should they have to do the bottom jobs? I even started to enjoy the details, meeting new people, and learning new districts.

A few months after my arrival, a firefighter named Doug transferred there. He was about my age, and we decided to take a trip to Jamaica. I moved some days around and had close to three weeks off. We drove to Miami, left my car at a Miami fire station, and flew to Jamaica.

Down in Jamaica, we found a hut to rent for ten bucks a night. We spent our days lying on the beach, drinking Red Stripe beer, and our nights listening to reggae music and drinking more Red Stripe beer. We even found a spot for lobster for five bucks.

On the drive back to Michigan, we ran into a huge snowstorm in Ohio. I was having a hard time driving my little yellow Beetle through the snow drifts. They ended up shutting down I-75 and made us wait in a rest area. I was starting to worry because I had to work the next morning. It was after 9:00 p.m. when we finally got back on the road and after 3:00 a.m. when I finally got to bed.

The next morning, I awoke and looked at the clock, nine thirty. That's got to be wrong. We start work at seven thirty, and if you're late, somebody calls you, and nobody called me. We had the buddy-relief system, which means a firefighter can't go home until his relief arrives. I ran to the kitchen, where the phone was, and to my horror, it was gone. While I was in Jamaica, I later found out, my roommate moved out and took the phone with him. I dressed as fast as I could, jumped in my car, and sped to work.

As soon as I walked in the back door of Ladder 22, I knew that I was in trouble. Ralph opened the door for me and said, "The captain already called the chief, and you're going down on charges!" I looked up at Ralph. He had a sad look on his face with a slight gleam in his eye. Darn, only a year on the job and I'm already going down on charges. This would be the first and, luckily, the only time that I would go down on charges.

In the army, they call it a court-martial, in the navy, it's a captain's mast, and in the Detroit Fire Department, it's called charges. It all means the same thing; you're in trouble. And just like the military, you put your dress uniform on and have a hearing in front of the base commander. For us, it's the chief of department.

My next workday, the captain and I drove down to Fire Department Headquarters. We went up to the chief of department's office. The chief of department's office was in the northwest corner of the third floor. His secretary told us to go right in. Sitting behind his desk was the chief of department.

He asked me how I pleaded, and I said, "Guilty."

He also asked, "Do you have anything to add?"

"No, sir," I responded. I didn't mention the blizzard; I just wanted to take my punishment.

Then my captain added, to my surprise, "Robert is a fine young man with a good attitude. He just made a mistake."

The chief sentenced me to serve two hours on my next leave day. That meant that on my next day off, I would be required to come in and work two hours. This was the practice back then; today, they dock your pay.

They also had sentences of long and short days for firemen who got into big trouble. Long and short days meant a firefighter had to come to work on his day off for twelve hours, short day, or for twenty-four hours, long day. A person receiving, say, ten long days would be required to stay at the engine house for the next ten days. That's ten days plus his regular workdays; he would not go home for sixteen days, no overtime. The court stopped the city from giving us long and short days. They referred to it as cruel and unusual punishment, which, I believe, is still illegal in the United States.

Many of the houses in the inner city are very old; some of them go back to the Civil War. Many were built without indoor plumbing. In later years, when they installed the indoor plumbing, they needed a room to put the bathroom fixtures in. Sometimes they would just wall off a hallway, add a door and bathroom fixtures, and call it a bathroom. This was usually the same hallway that had the doors to the basement and attic stairs and would cause problems for firefighters. First, it would be difficult to find the stairs in a fire, and second, some items placed in the attic or basement long ago could no longer be removed through the added bathroom fixtures.

One night, we had a small attic fire—still alarm engine and truck. I stretched the red line through the bathroom and up the narrow stairs and found the fire in the attic. Some old stuffed furniture and a mattress were burning; it was starting to get into the wall. I didn't have an air tank on; truck guys never wore them back then. The engine crew, all masked up, came up and started opening up the walls.

Normally, we would drag the mattress and furniture down the stairs, through the hallway, and out of the house. But in this old house, the hallway became the bathroom; there was no room to get the mattress and sofa through. Upstairs, it was getting pretty smoky. The engine crew asked me for the pipe, but no, you never give it up. I was squirting water on the burning stuffing as they chopped and pulled it apart. It was taking forever, and the smoke was getting worse and worse. It was getting harder and harder to breathe. Suddenly, I couldn't take it anymore, and I dove for the door. There were two guys on the stairs, and I went over both of them, rolling down to the bottom of the stairs.

"Are you all right?" my captain asked me.

Yeah, I'm all right, I thought as I threw up. I was more embarrassed than hurt. I hated those converted bathrooms.

A couple of weeks later, I went down another set of stairs. I was detailed to my old company, Engine 12. We had a second-story apartment on fire above a commercial building on Grand River. The entrance to the apartment was a single stairway with an entry street door. We busted the door. I stretched the one-and-a-half-inch line up the stairs; Tom Brink was behind me. There was a door at the top of the stairs, and behind it was a raging fire. I opened the door, and—*bam*—a back draft blew me into Tom, and I rode him like a sled on a snow hill all the way to the bottom. I got up and looked at Tom.

"Are you okay?" I asked.

"No, I think I might have broken my back," Tom replied.

I wanted to stay and assist Tom, but the building was on fire, and I had a job to do. The squad guys ran over and helped Tom. I went back up the stairs and put the fire out. When I came out, Tom was gone. They hauled him to the hospital. Tom injured his back, but it wasn't broke. It would be Tom's last day on the job. A couple of years later, I ran into Tom at the Box Bar in Plymouth, Michigan. He looked up and said, "You still owe me for the sled ride."

About a month later, we learned that Ladder 22 was getting a brand-new rig. This was something to get excited about. It was surprising that the department would give this sleepy old fire company a new fire truck. The one we had was a 1952 Seagrave with a sixty-five-foot aerial ladder and a gas motor. It could hardly keep up with traffic. The new one would be a Seagrave one-hundred-foot aerial, cab-forward design with a diesel motor. And most surprising, it would not be red. It would be painted a new color: lime green or slime green, as we called it.

The 1970s was a decade of change, and fire departments around the country did not want to be left out of the change action. One of the changes many of them made, including Detroit, was to change from the traditional color of fire-engine red to lime green.

Red is the traditional color of fire trucks. Firemen everywhere love red fire trucks. There is no more striking color to humans than red. That's why Mother Nature made our blood red. The first manufactured fire wagons back in the early 1800s were very expensive. So people wanted a bright and fancy color to show them off. They chose red, and two hundred years later, it's still the color of choice for fire departments.

The lime green color was started by a fire truck company. They were trying to figure a way to sell more fire trucks when an employee ran across a government study that said lime green was the most visible color at night. They painted a fire engine lime green and brought it to the annual fire equipment convention. Then they told people that soon the federal government would require all cities that received federal aid to switch to the new safer color. Of course, the government never did this. But the damage was done, and fire departments all over America soon switched colors. And our chiefs, who attended the convention, bought the story hook, line, and sinker.

Back at Ladder 22, we eagerly awaited the delivery of our new ladder truck, but as luck would have it, something else was delivered first: the transfer list. I was on it. I would be transferred to Engine 4, another slow company. I left just a couple of days before the new truck arrived. On my first day at Engine 4, I typed out a transfer request. I requested transfer to any busy company on the west side of the city. A few months later, they transferred me to Ladder 4, a fairly busy company that I would be in and out of for the rest of my career.

CHAPTER 7

I enjoyed my time at Ladder 4. It was a double house, and we usually ran with a minimum of nine firefighters, plenty of characters, and nonstop gags. Our captain was a nice guy whose number-one worry was losing tools at fires. Lose an axe or a pike pole at a fire and he went ballistic. So not to let him down, whenever we lost a tool on his off days, we would call him at home and let him know the bad news. His wife was very happy when he finally retired.

We had an engineer named Charley who was working two jobs to put his son through college. He didn't want his son to end up a loser fireman like the rest of us. When his son finally graduated and joined the fire department, we ribbed Charley so hard that he had to transfer out.

We had a tall guy named Darryl whose answer for anything asked was "My dick."

"Hey, Darryl, what are you doing?" I'd ask.

"My dick, that's what I'm doing."

"Darryl, what's for chow?" someone would ask.

"My dick, that's what's for chow."

No matter what was asked, the response was the same.

But the wildest of them all was a firefighter named Greg, who would end up being one of my best friends. Greg was a young guy, about my age, with a humorous smile and a hairline that started to recede in the second grade. Greg was arguably one of the best athletes on the job but unarguably the best practical joker on the job.

On my first day, we were fairly busy, up half the night. Around three in the morning, we were both hungry and scrounging for something to eat. The cook didn't leave us much. Greg found a box of oatmeal, porridge, he called it, and started to heat it up. He made enough for the whole house. It wasn't very good, and I said, "This oatmeal tastes like shit."

"Yeah, well, you look like shit," he responded and flung a spoonful of oatmeal in my direction. I lobbed my oatmeal at him, and back and forth we went. Oatmeal was flying in every way. It was on the walls, on the ceiling, cupboards, tables, you name it.

We didn't stop until the entire pot was empty then laughed and continued our conversation for another hour or so. When finished, we decided to clean up our mess. A little tip; do not let oatmeal harden. We had ladders and buckets and chisels and a pile of red death, the department's famous cleaning powder. We were still cleaning when the other unit arrived.

"What the heck did you two idiots do?" asked the incoming lieutenant.

"Just spilled a little oatmeal, sir," we told him.

A fun thing about running here was the tiller truck, that long fire truck with a fireman steering the back end. I learned to tiller right away, hands on the top of the steering wheel when going forward and hands on the bottom of the steering wheel when backing up. We all wanted to tiller and would fight for the tiller bucket. Then a new opportunity arose. The department started a position called DA, short for driver applicant.

It takes five years to reach full pay, but if you had two years on the job, you could put in for DA. Driver applicants filled in for drivers. Every day you drove, you would get full driver's pay, which was a nice pay raise. I typed a letter requesting DA. On my next workday, and to my surprise, I was detailed to Ladder 21 to drive.

Ladder 21 was the busiest ladder truck in the city at that time. They had a new one-hundred-foot American LaFrance tiller rig. I walked in and found the officer and explained to him that this was my first day as a DA and that I had never driven a fire truck before, not the front end anyway.

"What!" he screamed. "This is BS. No way are you driving my rig."

"Take it easy, lieutenant," one of the deckies said. "We'll teach him." And teach me they did. We went out in the morning with me in the front seat, driving, and drove around. We had a dozen fire runs that day, and nothing bad happened. It's not an easy task driving on some of the narrow side streets of Detroit.

They had me speeding down main streets, like Livernois and Grand River. I was going through red lights with the sirens blaring. Then I was backing into tight, narrow quarters that were designed for horses. I did it all, and all was done successfully. Even the chief got into the fun. He parked his car right next to the engine house door that I had to back into. No problem. So that was it; I was a driver, at least for the next few years. There are drivers and firefighters, although both fight fires. The macho nachos usually skipped the driver's job for two reasons. One, they didn't want to take details. They usually were the guys that were sent to a good spot and never transferred out. Two, they hoped to become a super firefighter and eventually run on a busy squad company.

Fire department squads or heavy squads or flying squads were invented by the Detroit Fire Department over a hundred years ago. Detroit's squad companies were our special forces, the busiest fire companies in Detroit, maybe in the world. Back in the early seventies, Detroit had fifty engine companies and thirty truck companies but only nine squad companies. Nowadays, it's down to six. The city sent at least one squad to every fire, so the average squad company did twice the fire service of an engine or truck company. Also, the squad guys painted their helmets red. Back then, we all wore black helmets, except for the chiefs, who wore white. The squad guys stood out.

But I was happy doing what I was doing, being a DA, learning the city, learning how to drive the different rigs, tiller trucks, straight trucks, and squads. I drove them all. I even drove the department ambulance and the boat tender. The boat tender was a heavy-duty

GMC truck with two huge water cannons on the back end. The water cannons were metal works of art over one hundred years old. The boat tender responded to all multiple-alarm fires. The ambulance was a custom-built rig with a full operating room inside. It also would respond to all multiple-alarm fires in case a firefighter was injured.

The squad rigs at the time were all enclosed rigs. They kind of looked like a short, red school bus. They were designed to carry special equipment, such as the Jaws of Life, and to be able to transport injured people to the hospital.

Most of our rigs in the early seventies were old and falling apart. It would be a miracle just to get them to the fire. The repair shop would be called two or three times a day for repairs. Some of the rigs were over twenty-five years old. They had old twelve-cylinder gas engines, and they were all manual transmission. Many had to be double-clutched. To double-clutch meant, instead of shifting from second gear to third gear, you had to shift to neutral, take your foot off the clutch, then repress the clutch and shift gears. There was no power steering or power brakes.

You would find yourself driving a ladder truck down some narrow street as fast as possible, shifting and steering and watching out for traffic, and all the while, the boss is screaming in your ear, "Don't lose the engine." The squads were the worst. The interior was open so the firefighters in the back would join in on the screaming.

"Let's go, kid. Jesus Christ, did you ever drive before?"

One of my more embarrassing experiences happened on a detail to ladder 26. Ladder 26 is on the far northwest side of Detroit. One of the streets in its district is called Telegraph. Telegraph is a six-lane highway with grassy medians in the middle. Its traffic lights are a mile apart. Growing up in the sixties, Telegraph was our local drag strip. There was nothing like it during the sixties. Detroit was a rich town, jobs were everywhere, and every kid eighteen or older had a good job and a new fast car.

American cars in the sixties came ready to drag race: Road Runners, 442s, SS-396, Boss Mustangs, and my favorite, GTOs. I had a 1968 GTO and spent every moment I could racing down Telegraph and cruising the drive-ins. I had over thirty points on my driver's record. Most of my tickets were from drag racing on Telegraph.

So just a couple of years after I stopped drag racing on Telegraph, I was detailed to Ladder 26. The rig was a twenty-year-old, beat-up Seagrave tiller truck with a bad clutch. The repair shop came out and adjusted it the best they could. There were no X rigs (replacement rigs). The fastest the rig could do was twenty miles an hour.

It was a Saturday night, about ten, and we had a box alarm that took us right down Telegraph. The street, as usual, was packed with drag racers. Then there we came, lights on, sirens blaring, and only going twenty miles an hour. How ironic, after all the years I spent on this street, speeding, racing, breaking all the laws, and then when I could speed legally, I can't even do the speed limit. Folks were beeping horns, passing me up. Even some old lady driving a Ford Falcon with a Kleenex box on the dashboard yelled for us to get out of the way. Yes, that was an embarrassing night.

A driver required many skills other than driving. One of them was being a bump-and-paint man. The last thing I ever wanted to happen to me was to go down on charges for an accident. Even though our old rigs were falling apart, if I put a dent on one, it could cost me twelve hours' pay. Three accidents and I would never drive again. So I did my best to avoid accidents, and if that wasn't possible, I did my best to cover them up and avoid going down on charges.

One night, we had a second alarm on the boulevard, a three-story apartment going from top to bottom. Chief Nelson was in charge, a hard-charging chief who kept his cool at fires. The worst kinds of chiefs were what we called screamers, chiefs that ran around, screaming orders that usually nobody listened to. Chief Nelson was one of the only chiefs back then that would give the order "Let it burn. Just protect the exposures." I liked that. Why risk our lives over a vacant building?

But this apartment was too big to let burn. Chief Nelson ordered me to take Ladder 4 around the rear of the building and set up a water tower. The only problem was the street was blocked with parked cars. He had me squeeze between two cars and run over a no-parking sign to get to the rear. I did as was ordered, and I smashed the right fender while driving over the sign. In most departments, I wouldn't be in trouble, but not in Detroit.

When we got back to quarters, we gathered around the rig to assess the damage. The lieutenant said that I should put a letter in about the accident. But that would mean that I would end up going down on charges.

"Come on, Lieutenant," I said, "let me try to fix it."

"All right," he said, "as long as it's finished before the captain gets in."

Our captain always went by the rule book. He was on a mission to keep our quarters and rigs perfect. This accident and cover-up wouldn't go down well. He was due in at 0700 hours. And it was now 0400 hours.

Greg and the boys stayed up the rest of the night with me. Using makeshift tools, we bent and hammered away at the solid-steel fender until it was pretty straight. I was putting on a second coat of red paint (a staple in every fire station) when a voice behind me asked, "What are you doing?"

"Trying to get this fender fixed before the captain gets in," I answered. I turned around to look at the voice behind me, and it was the captain. He just gave me a disappointed look and walked away. I felt pretty bad, but it was better than losing twelve hours' pay.

Repairing the rigs is a way of life in Detroit fire stations. Drive by a fire station in the middle of the night and hear pounding and banging and you can guess that they probably hit something. The old barns we run out of were originally designed for horses, not the huge rigs we use today. The apparatus doors allow only three inches clearance on each side. Big accidents or accidents involving life or property, of course, we always report. But the small ones, we try to take care of ourselves, and we feel we're saving the city some money too.

This is one advantage to having an old, seasoned rig as opposed to a new one. A new rig, you get in trouble for every scratch. After a few years, and the city keeps fire trucks in service for at least twenty, it's hard to tell the new dents from the old.

A few years back, some guys on the east side got into trouble over a minor accident. Their ladder hit a civilian vehicle. It was minor damage to the car and no damage to the fire truck. The car was a fifteen-year-old, beat-up piece of junk. The firemen offered to pay the guy one hundred dollars cash out of their own pockets instead of making a police report. He initially agreed, and then later he had a change of heart and went to the media with the story. The media loved the story. Firemen Involved in a Hit-and-Run Accident Then Offer Hush Money. They got away with calling it a hit-and-run because, technically, all accidents are supposed to be reported to the police.

It turned out that the civilian didn't have a license or insurance or proper license plates, among other things. It wasn't even his car. But guess who got in trouble? Not the civilian! The firemen did. All that they were doing was trying to save themselves and the city a little money and grief. Sometimes you just can't win.

CHAPTER 8

1974

The year 1974 was the year of the big change for Detroit. It was the year Detroit went from two hundred years of whites running the town to black rule. I look at what Detroit went through back then as a revolution, a revolution that the blacks won fair and square. Every revolution has a hero and Detroit's was Coleman A. Young.

Coleman Young was as great a revolutionary leader as there ever was. Fidel Castro, Che Guevara, you name them, none can top Detroit's Coleman Young. Coleman was born in Alabama. In the 1920s, his folks moved to Detroit, where he was raised. In the late 1930s, he worked for the Ford Motor Company, where he was fired for union activities. During World War II, he served with the Tuskegee Airmen, where he was a leader in the infamous Freeman Field Mutiny. After the war, he joined the Communist Party and was called before the Senate during the McCarthy hearings on un-American activities, where he refused to testify. In 1964, he was elected to the Michigan Senate, and ten years later, he became Detroit's first black mayor, replacing Roman Gribbs.

Coleman defeated John S. Nichols in the most polarizing election Detroit ever had. Nichols was Detroit's police commissioner. A World War II vet who wore his hair in a crew cut and carried a pearl-handled pistol. He had started a new program called STRESS, which stood for "Stop the robbers eventually save the streets." And depending upon who you talked to, it was a great success or a terror to the city. The whites loved it, and the blacks hated it.

In Coleman Young's victory speech, he told the crooks to hit Eight Mile, Detroit's legendary northern border. But many of the whites that were in the city didn't believe he meant the crooks, he meant them, and they went. Detroit's population, which peaked at almost two million in the 1950s, dropped to below a million during Young's last term in office. Whites left the city in droves. The revolution was over, and the whites had lost.

If the revolution ended with Young's victory, it started seven years earlier on a hot July night, Detroit's riot. It was July 1967, five years before I joined the department. I was just a seventeen-year-old teenager living on the far west side and had no idea what was happening. Later, after joining the department, the older guys would tell us stories of that week in July, when they fought two thousand fires in five days.

When it happened, the Detroit riot was the largest riot ever in America. All off-duty firefighters were called in and were not allowed to go home for five days. The governor ordered forty-seven different suburbs to send in their fire crews. Two Detroit firefighters were killed, and hundreds were injured.

The irony was that, back in 1967, Detroiters, blacks included, enjoyed one of the highest incomes and one of the highest rates of home ownership in America. Riots, or racial insurrections, were happening all over America, but our leaders, including Detroit's Mayor Cavanagh, who the black community overwhelmingly supported, thought a riot would never happen in Detroit. Boy, were they wrong.

The riot started on a hot July Saturday night. The police raided a blind pig on Twelfth Street, and within two hours, a crowd of a couple hundred people showed up and started pelting the police with rocks and bottles. The Detroit Police had devised a plan to use in case of a racial insurrection called Show the Flag. That plan is still studied in colleges all over America and thought to be the worst plan ever. The plan basically was to send a lot of police to the scene and have them just stand by and do nothing, thinking that just a show of force would scare people and they would go home.

Well, they didn't go home, and instead, they looted stores and shot people and burned down buildings. And the police and firemen couldn't go home either. The governor sent in the Michigan National Guard, and the president sent in the US Army's Eighty-Second Division. It took an entire week before things returned to normal. But things never really did return to normal.

I experienced a crazy event one hot July night during the riot. A friend named Mike and I were visiting another friend named Red, who lived on Washburn, just south of Grand River. We were all Detroit teenagers. The three of us thought that we would experience the riot. We walked up to the corner, found a ledge to sit on, talked, and drank bottles of ice-cold Pepsi. There was a curfew on, and Grand River, a very lively street at the time, was completely still, not a car or a soul on it. I had never seen anything like it. We must have sat there for an hour.

Unexpectedly, Red, who worked for the railroad, went home and returned with a railroad flare. Then for some reason, which I will never figure out even if I live to be a hundred, he lit it and threw it out on Grand River.

Out of nowhere, an army jeep started up its motor and came after us. We started to run. We ran around the corner toward Red's house. Red made a right and ran down the alley, Mike kept going straight, and I jumped behind the bushes of the first house. The jeep stopped right in front of the house, and I heard a voice with a southern drawl say, "All right, boy, I'm not screwing around. I'm counting to three and shooting right into that bush. One, two—"

"Don't shoot, don't shoot, I'm coming out!" I said.

The soldier grabbed me, threw me to the ground, and proceeded to kick the crap out of me. He then held his rifle to my head and said, "Give me one good reason why I shouldn't blow your head off?"

"Please don't shoot me" was all I could say.

"Well, all right, get up and go home," the soldier said.

"I can't walk," I said.

"Then crawl home."

Crawl home was what I did. I could not walk because of the severe beating. Red, who ran down the alley, got caught climbing a fence. The soldiers poked him a few times in his back with their bayonets as he hung on the fence. We used to wear plain white T-shirts back then. The back of his shirt was the same color as his name. Mike, who ran straight, got away.

They say no American city ever really recovers from a riot, and Detroit is living proof. In the years that followed the riot, the city just went downhill. Nobody went downtown anymore, so the stores either closed down or moved out. Crime was out of control, fires unheard of a few years back were commonplace, and people were afraid to walk the streets. Cops were getting shot, and firemen were getting attacked. The revolution was on, and the whites left in droves. People called it White Flight.

Then, in 1974, Coleman A. Young became our mayor. Also, that same year, a new city charter went into effect, changing the top person of the fire department from the chief of department to an appointed commissioner. On June 26, 1974, Melvin Jefferson, a black businessman, became our first commissioner and our first black leader. He replaced Joseph Deneweth, who would probably be the last white supervisor of the department.

I look back at those years with bewilderment. The Detroit of my youth, during the 1950s and the 1960s, was a magical place, the best city in the world, we believed! We pitied folks who lived in other cities, like New York and Chicago. Detroiters lived on treelined streets in nice homes with garages in the back and new cars parked inside. We had the best schools, the best parks, a beautiful downtown, and low crime.

That all started to change about the time of the riot. The crime and murder rate started soaring as the population began to rapidly decline. Less people, less jobs, less money, and more crime, Detroit was becoming a less desirable place to live. Words like *bussing, open housing, the Black Panthers,* and *declining property values* were all anybody was talking about. By the time Coleman Young showed up, Detroit was in decline, and unfortunately, he did little to reverse it.

March of 1974, a firefighter named Ed Gargol was killed. He was responding to a box alarm on Ladder 26. Ladder 26 made a sharp right turn at Grand River and Burt Road. Ed was strapping on his MSA air tank. Usually, the truck guys didn't put on air tanks on the way to a fire. Their job was to ventilate, and the bulky air tanks just got in the way, but Central reported that there were people trapped. When we hear that, everyone tanks up. When Ladder 26 turned, Ed lost control and fell off the rig, hitting his head on the pavement. He died immediately.

Ed was short with dark hair slicked back, an Elvis-looking guy, that is if Elvis was a badass, which Ed certainly was. He was the same age as me and hung out at the same neighborhood bar that I did, the First Edition Lounge. Ed wasn't from my neighborhood, but for some reason, he chose to hang out with us. He even started dating Sandy, one of the local girls. Their relationship, like many relationships, had its ups and downs, and Sandy was one to let you know if she and Ed were having problems. And to make matters worse, about a week before Ed was killed, he got into a huge fistfight with one of my old neighborhood friends.

Ed was one of those guys who lived on the edge, the kind who climbed mountains or jumped out of planes or swam with the sharks. And like most people who live on the edge, he was always stirring up a little controversy. Because I was a Detroit fireman like Ed, the crowd at the bar would always lump us together. Every night, it seemed someone told me another Ed Gargol story. The night I entered the bar, I was prepared to hear another one.

When Ed was killed, I was off duty, and I didn't know anything about it. The next night, when I stopped in the First Edition, the first person I ran into was an off-duty firefighter named Jim, who wasn't a regular at the bar.

"Hey, Bob," he said, "you probably haven't heard, having been off duty, but a fireman got killed last night. His name was Ed Gargol!"

I felt like I had just gotten punched in the gut. I was in shock and was very confused. Slowly, I left Jim and found a place alone at the end of the bar. I had to try to think things out. Of all the crazy things, I thought, why this? Poor Ed! I couldn't believe that he was dead, another great Detroit firefighter who was heartbreakingly gone.

As I was sitting alone, brooding, I heard someone say "Bob." I looked up, and standing there was Sandy, Ed's girlfriend. I looked up at her and said, "Ed."

"I don't ever want to hear that name again," Sandy said. "Ed was supposed to meet me here tonight, and where is he? I'm sick of this shit."

"You don't know?" I asked.

"Don't know what?" she replied.

"Ed's dead!" I said. "Ed's dead. He was killed last night. He fell off the truck, responding to a house fire. He hit his head and died."

She just stood there frozen. She looked at me straight in the eyes with an "if looks could kill" look. There she stood, staring at me, not saying a word. After a long minute, she turned and ran straight out the door. I called out to her, but she just kept running. I ran outside and looked for her in the parking lot, but she was gone.

Looking back, I often wondered how I could have handled that situation differently. They teach you a lot of things in the academy, but how to tell a person her firefighter boyfriend was just killed isn't one of them. Sandy was at the funeral and funeral home every moment it was open, doing all she could and helping the family. When the funeral home wasn't open, she went door-to-door, collecting money to help pay the funeral expenses.

After that, we didn't see much of Sandy. She stopped coming to the bar. She must have taken it pretty bad. Of all the things I learned in life, how to handle a firefighter's death with their loved ones just isn't one of them.

CHAPTER 9

The Detroit Fireman's Field Day was a colossal annual event that the Detroit Fire Department put on every summer. It was held at Tiger Stadium. We would raffle off a dozen new cars. Every fireman sold Fireman's Field Day tickets. Some of us would sell thousands of them. The event itself was a fun event. It was always held on a Sunday and lasted as long as three hours. Over half of the fire trucks in the city, the new ones without dents, would be there on parade. We had a Detroit Fire Department band that would march around while playing music. We had old fire trucks performing, including the ones pulled by horses. The Thrill Team, east side versus west side, would challenge each other in death-defying maneuvers. And last but not least, we had our celebrated Detroit Fire Department Clown Team.

The first time I saw the clowns perform at the Field Day I knew that I wanted to join them. They were hilarious, performing professional clown skits. They looked as good as any circus clowns. They had their own clown team fire truck donated by Ford Motor Company in 1958, and it's still running. They were the stars of the show.

Shortly after the Field Day, Greg, who also wanted to join the clown team, and I put letters in requesting to join the team. About six months later, Dennis Lawrence, then the head of the clown team, invited us to a meeting held at night at the academy. We both went, and that was it for the next fifteen years. We were two DFD clowns.

The first thing we learned was how to put makeup on our faces. There are three types of clown faces—whiteface, tramp, and auguste. Auguste is what I chose. They paint their faces reddish orange with white around the mouth and eyes. I had a friend of mine make me a patched tramp outfit, and I found a shoemaker who made me a big pair of red clown shoes. I was ready. I even registered my name, Bobo the Hobo, with Clowns of America.

We performed everywhere—schools, hospitals, and orphanages. We were some of the best PR the Detroit Fire Department ever had. Politicians would request us for their kids' birthday parties. Every year, we would do a Christmas show at the Northville State Sanatorium before they closed it down. It was one of the hardest and saddest things I ever did.

They divide the children into three groups according to their condition. The third group was the most severe. They were the ones that we would put the show on for. It would be so hard to stay and not leave the room for three hours. Those poor children could get very messy. But we never left the room, no matter how difficult it was. There are few people in this world that I have more respect for than the people who work with those children. Being there would put us in the Christmas spirit.

Almost every parade in the Detroit area requested the clown team. Our old clown fire truck would come down the street, making silly noises while belching smoke. The driver would speed up to the crowd, slam on the brakes, and we would come rolling off the roof, slamming the pavement. The crowd would go nuts. I think that I have more arthritis pain from clown team maneuvers than from fire injuries. The strange thing was that one parade that we weren't in was the Detroit Thanksgiving Day Parade.

The Thanksgiving Parade is the biggest parade in Detroit. It's nationally televised. It comes down Woodward Avenue on Thanksgiving morning, and close to a million people show up to watch. It's a Detroit tradition. Engine 5, a fire station right off the parade route, throws a big party for all the DFD kids, complete with cookies and hot cocoa. The clowns would be there to entertain the kids. But we weren't in the parade. Nobody knew why.

At the time, the parade was called the JL Hudson Parade, sponsored by the now-defunct department store. I investigated why we weren't in the big parade. I found out that we used to be in the parade back in the fifties. I contacted the people at Hudson's that ran the parade and offered our services; they were delighted to have us back in their parade. From then on, every Thanksgiving to this very day, the DFD Clown Team has been a big part of the parade, national TV and all.

Boblo Island was an amusement park on the Detroit River twenty miles south of Detroit. It was a place every Detroit kid used to go to. To get there, you took the Boblo boat from Downtown Detroit. Greeting every kid as he or she walked on the boat was Captain Boblo, a little person who wore a ship captain's uniform. Every Detroiter knew Captain Boblo. When he died, they asked the DFD Clown Team to be his pallbearers. The local news crews covered the funeral. I had more friends see me on TV as Captains Boblo's pallbearer than any fire I ever went to.

But the main show was always the Fireman's Field Day at Tiger Stadium. The clowns would put on world-renowned skits, just like the circus. We loved the Field Day. Too bad it had to end, and end it did. A big reason it ended had to do with just one fireman who I shall call Wally April.

Fireman's Field Day tickets came in books of twenty-five, and you sold them for a dollar apiece. As an incentive, they let you keep a couple of dollars from every book you sold. Wally was a great ticket salesman. He would sell thousands. Wally talked the Detroit Firemen's Fund, who ran the Field Day, into giving him a bigger commission. The more tickets he sold, the bigger his commission grew and grew. The fund then bought the new prize cars that they were giving away early so the top ticket sellers, including Wally, could use them to sell more tickets.

On the day of the Field Day, Wally, always the showman, showed up fashionably late. He was holding huge garbage bags containing all the ticket stubs he sold. Some of the winners had already been drawn, and many in the crowd, seeing that their ticket stubs weren't in the barrel, got angry. The fund was forced to redraw. The next day, the media reported that the winner of a new Lincoln claimed that it wasn't new. It had thousands of miles on it and cigarette burns and litter under the seats. Then word leaked out to the firemen that Wally got this huge commission for selling all those tickets. The guys were so mad that most said that they would never sell tickets again.

Well, that was it for the old Fireman's Field Day. They have a small one now mainly for firemen and their families. The clown team is still going as strong as ever; hopefully, it will be with us for years and years. I just was glad that Wally was never a clown.

On a hot July Sunday afternoon, the chief called and asked if I could drive an engine for a couple of hours. "Sure," I said. He sent me east to Engine 36. The FEO had to go home for a couple hours. When I got there, he showed me how to operate the rig. Engine 36 had a snorkel-type contraption on it. "Don't worry," he said, "it doesn't work." As soon as he left, we had a box alarm and off we went. It was about a ten-block run.

When we pulled up, we saw that we had a grocery store on fire, and there were about a hundred people standing around, waiting for the show to begin on this hot afternoon. I pulled up to the hydrant on the corner and began to hook up the soft suction. The guys on the back were stretching line to the front of the store. Two guys from the truck ran to the rear of the store to bust open the back door.

Using a Halligan bar and a large crowbar, they struggled to open the steel door. The crowd was watching in anticipation. Stored against the back door were stacks of canned vegetables, yellow corn, green peas, and so on. When the firemen popped the door open, all the cans went rolling into the alley. The crowd immediately went after the cans. It was crazy!

But once they found out that the cans were canned vegetables, their excitement turned to anger. I guess they were hoping for something better. The crowd started throwing the loose cans, first at the two firemen, who were now running for their lives, then at me. I was all by myself at the hydrant when they started throwing cans in my direction. One can broke the right side window as I was hooking up the two-and-a-half and trying to play away with the water. I jumped under the rig, scared shitless. Cans were hitting everywhere. Then I started to hear a police siren.

A blue police car pulled up. They were blue back then, and two cops jumped out. One cop had a long wooden club, and the other had a big flashlight, and they both charged the crowd. Never, ever would I underestimate the courage of the Detroit Police, especially back then. It was like two cops charging a hundred people as if it were a hundred cops charging just two people. They ran in headfirst, swinging their clubs. People started backing up, and some started to run away. Within a couple of minutes, they had the crowd under control. Nowadays, they probably would be parked down the street, waiting for a SWAT team.

After the fire was out, when we backed back into quarters, I noticed that the FEO had returned and was waiting for me. He looked at the damaged window that I had taped up with white medical tape.

"What the heck did you do to my rig?" he said.

"Hey, I'm sorry," I told him, "but they gave me a couple cans of corn."

A couple weeks later, I was rummaging through a yard sale, and I came across an old copy of the book *Europe on Ten Dollars a Day*. I brought it to the enginehouse and showed it to my friend Greg. "We should do it," he said. I agreed and began to plan for a trip to Europe. We were both about twenty-five years old and figured that it was time for us to see the world.

We got time off from work through furloughs and work reliefs and gathered every cent we could muster and bought our tickets. We flew KLM Airlines to Amsterdam. We bought a Eurail pass and traveled by train everywhere.

One night, we were sitting in a bar in Amsterdam, talking to the barmaid. We were telling her that we were firemen in America, and this guy jumped up from his barstool and said, "My name is Hans. I too am a fireman for the city of Amsterdam." He joined us for a beer and told us that tomorrow was the one hundredth anniversary of the Amsterdam Fire Department.

"You must join me," he said.

We said," sure," and told him where we were staying.

The next morning, at eight sharp, Hans was there, banging on our door. The three of us, Greg, Hans, and I, piled into Hans's car, the littlest car I had ever seen, and off we went. Our first stop was Hans's Amsterdam fire station. It was a modern two-story building with bay doors lining the front, enough for about ten fire trucks. The second story was lined with windows and looked like it must contain offices and dorm rooms.

Once inside, Hans introduced us to everybody. They seemed excited to meet American firemen. They told us that they rode eight men on an engine and two on a truck. Each person on the engine had a number, and according to your number, you had an assigned task to perform at the fire. The number 1 and 2 men hooked up the hoses, which were all detached. The number 3 and 4 men stretched the lines into the structure, and 5 and 6 ventilated and did rescue. It was a lot different than the freelance we did in Detroit.

What was really different was their fire gear. They wore wool fire pants and wool fire coats, leather boots, and a helmet that looked like something the French wore during World War I, not the rubber and Nomex gear we had in the United States. Their breathing apparatus was pretty strange too. Instead of full facepieces, they wore goggles and mouth covers, like what patients wear during operations.

But strangest of all were the poles they slid down on; instead of brass, like the fire poles in the United States, their poles were made of wood, thick wood poles about six inches in diameter covered with a glossy varnish finish. I asked Hans if he ever got slivers sliding down those wood poles. "No," he said, "we just keep a lot of varnish on them."

Our next stop was the Amsterdam Fire Museum. It was an old brick fire station in the center of a city park. Inside, it had all the things you would expect—old fire trucks, old uniforms, historical fire pictures, and an old Gamewell telegraph system. When we asked about it, Hans told us that they used the Gamewell system before the war to dispatch their runs. When we told him that we had the same exact system in Detroit and we still used it to get our runs, he started to laugh. "You Americans," he said, "always making jokes." I wish we were, I thought.

Next, we went to Hans's apartment to pick up his wife, Katrina. When we got there and met Katrina, Greg and I almost fell over. Katrina looked like a movie star with her long, blond hair and her shiny black leather coat. The four of us loaded into Hans's little car. First, we stopped at a Chinese restaurant for dinner then off to a fire station where they were putting on a show for their one hundredth anniversary.

The fire station where the show was going on looked a lot like Engine 5 in Detroit, except that it had a canal next to it. On the canal was a Dutch fireboat squirting water. Covering the whole fire station were white bedsheets that they lit on fire. As the flames spread, firemen dressed like women, came to the windows, and began screaming for help. This was before there were women firefighters. Soon, other firemen were climbing up ladders, holding nets and rescuing the women. It was a great show, and hundreds of people watched and cheered.

While all this was going on, Hans was listening to the fire radio, and then he said to us, "There are three classes of fires in Amsterdam: big fires, medium fires, and small fires, and right now on the radio, there is a big fire going on. Would you like to go?"

"Hell yes," we said. And the four of us piled into Hans's little car and headed to the big fire.

When we got to the fire, I was amazed. They had a huge waterfront warehouse going throughout; fire was shooting out the roof up to the stars. The building looked to be hundreds of years old, probably from the old Dutch traders. Dutch firemen were running back and forth in their wool uniforms and French Army helmets. They were busy unrolling hoses, raising aerial ladders, battling this out-of-control blaze. This fire would be a 4-alarm fire in Detroit.

Katrina, who, like the rest of us, was trying to avoid the water spray and stay warm in her shiny leather, looked at me and said, "I never saw a fire before."

"Most firemen's wives never see a fire. They just think that we play checkers all day," I told her.

"Not me," she said. "I thought Hans just played chess all day." We both laughed.

After a couple hours of watching the fire, we decided it was time to go. The four of us squeezed into Hans's little car and headed for home. They dropped us off at our hotel, and we thanked him for a wonderful day. Greg and I agreed that you could never get a better tour of a fire department than the one we just had. That night, as I lay in bed, I thought of how lucky I was to be a firefighter. You can go anywhere in the world and they have fires and they have firefighters. We are a worldwide brotherhood, and what a great world that is.

CHAPTER 10

When we returned to Detroit, there was a new word going around the firehouse: *layoff*. It was a word I thought I would never hear as a fireman because firemen never got laid off, or so we thought.

Most people who take government jobs, join the fire department or the police department, do it for the security. We know that we won't get rich like people do in the business world, but we don't care. We just want a steady job with a steady paycheck and, hopefully, a pension and benefits. I know it's ironic that people with some of the most dangerous jobs, cops and firemen, do them for the security, but that's the way it is. So you can imagine what a shock it was to us when we learned that the city planned to lay off around three hundred of us.

Mayor Coleman Young told us the city was broke and offered us a deal, layoffs or pay cuts. The union organized a big meeting where we would vote on whether to take a layoff or take a pay cut. The argument against the pay cuts was "Do you trust the mayor? We will take the pay cuts, and he will lay us off anyway." This actually proved to be true to the police who agreed to take pay cuts. The mayor still laid them off.

Another factor for consideration was where you were on the seniority list. Everything in the Detroit Fire Department, from promotions to layoffs, went by strict seniority, and there was no reason to think that this would be any different. At the time, I was over four hundred from the bottom, so a layoff of three hundred shouldn't affect me, or so I thought.

The union meeting was packed, standing room only. The arguments went back and forth whether to take pay cuts or layoffs, but not surprisingly, the majority favored layoffs. Soon, the question was called, and it was time to vote.

Just before the vote, a brother raised his hand and asked this question: "Is the layoff going to be strict seniority?" *Of course, it's going to be strict seniority*, I thought. *Everything is strict seniority. What a dumb question.* But to my amazement, Earl Berry, our union president, didn't say that; instead, he looked down from his podium and cautiously said, "Yeah, it will be seniority, except for a couple of people who have prior city time."

What, I thought, *a couple of people who have prior city time! What the heck does that mean?* I knew that something unusual was going on. Strangely enough, I think that I was the only one in the entire union hall who heard it or who understood it. The vote went as expected; layoffs, not pay cuts, would rule the moment. The meeting ended, and Earl Berry prepared to leave.

I tried raising my hand to ask the question, but they wouldn't call on me. I tried to talk to Earl Berry, but he avoided me. Finally, I stood and blocked the exit door as Earl approached.

"You can't leave until you answer just one question," I said.

"What's your question?" he said.

"What did you mean 'a couple who have prior city time'?" I asked.

"When did you come on?"

"June 1972," I told him.

"Tomorrow you're getting laid off," Earl said as he walked out the door.

I was in shock. I drove to the Cartwheel Bar on Grand River, where everyone was headed. When I walked in, I saw that the boys were in a jovial mood. And why shouldn't they be? They weren't getting laid off, so they thought, and their paychecks wouldn't be cut. When I told them that something strange was going on and tomorrow we would be laid off, they almost fell over laughing. "What's wrong with you, Dombrowski? Layoffs go by seniority, just like everything else on the department," they said. I tried to explain it to them, but it was no use. I ended up betting every one of them, including my classmate Larry, five bucks apiece, that tomorrow we would be laid off.

The next day, as luck would have it, I was detailed to another fire station, Ladder 9. Larry, my old classmate buddy, ran there. About five in the afternoon, the chief came by with layoff notices. "Dombrowski," he said, "sorry, I have a layoff notice for you." He then looked at Larry and said, "I got one for you too." Larry reached in his pocket and handed me my five bucks.

I was not going to take this sitting down! Why was I being laid off when people with less seniority weren't? I went to the union, but they were no help. They claimed that they didn't know what was going on. So I went looking for a lawyer.

I went downtown to the Detroit Bar Association. At the time, they offered a wonderful service. For fifteen dollars, you would get one hour with a lawyer who specializes in your problem. They sent me to the top of the Penobscot Building, one of Detroit's tallest buildings, to talk to one of Detroit's best labor lawyers. There, the lawyer explained to me that the layoff list, fair or unfair, was agreed on by the union, and there was nothing I could do about it. I would have to sue the union and would have no chance of winning. Kicked out by the city and sold out by the union, and nothing I could do—those were my thoughts as I walked out of the lawyer's office.

We were soon to learn this layoff was going to take another interesting turn. My old classmate Bigley, who was spending his time as a firefighter, decided that it was time to make his move in the New Detroit. He went to federal court and filed a lawsuit stopping the city from laying off black firefighters, just the white guys. This went over like a lead balloon with the white firefighters. Suddenly, Mark Bigley became the most hated guy on the department, at least among the whites.

In Detroit, everything comes down to race. President Berry must have anticipated this. When we had our day in court and the layoff list was broken down, half the layoffs went to blacks and half went to whites. The judge sided with the union and tossed the case out. Most of the members who did receive prior city time were blacks who transferred to the fire department from other city departments, like the DSR or the DPW. Had the union not allowed prior city time, the vast majority of the layoffs would have been black firefighters instead of half white and half black. Bigley might have won his case instead of losing it. Earl Berry was a pretty sharp union leader.

The victory was bittersweet for I was still to be laid off, but I would be called back a little quicker. I stopped Bigley at the courthouse and asked him what the hell he was doing.

"I'm just trying to stop all the layoffs," he said.

"Bullshit," I replied.

Well, if Detroit didn't want us, Houston did. Houston, Texas, when they heard about our layoff, called and offered us jobs in their fire department. It was the seventies, the first of the new American migration going south. Thousands of Michigan residents who lost jobs in the auto plants packed up and headed down to the new promised land. Texas, with the oil embargo and high oil prices, was booming. We were called the black tags because of the black color of the Michigan license plates.

Al, one of the laid-off Detroit firefighters, owned a motor home. Five of us, including Al, packed it up and headed south to Houston. When we got there, we found out that it was a trick. Houston wasn't looking for firemen. They were looking for cops.

At the time, Houston had a two-thousand-man fire department and a two-thousand-man police department. The new mayor wanted to double the police department. They were looking for guys from the north who didn't wear cowboy boots and cowboy hats. Their city was growing, and they wanted a new cosmopolitan image. They told us that we would be perfect. Sorry, we told them, we were firemen, not cops.

A funny thing happened while we were there. We were sitting in the waiting room of the Houston Fire Department Recruiting Office, and a well-dressed black guy came in. He reached in his pocket to give the receptionist his card, and something fell out. After he left, I looked around the carpet and found a marijuana joint, if you can believe it. I picked it up and ran out to the hallway, but he was gone. I looked up and down the halls, but he was nowhere. Finally, I looked out a hallway window, and I could see him in the parking lot, walking to his car. I ran down the stairs and out to the lot, stopped him, and gave him his joint.

"Whoa, what's that?" he asked.

"A marijuana joint that just fell out of your pocket," I told him.

"No, man, that's not mine," he said.

"Yeah, it is. Look, I don't give a shit. I'm from Detroit," I said.

He thanked me and told me that he was glad I, and not somebody else, had found it. He then asked me what I was doing there, and I told him. "Well, this is your lucky day," he said. He explained to me that he worked for the government and went wherever cities were hiring firefighters to make sure that they weren't discriminating against minorities.

"Did you ever hear of Tacoma, Washington?" he asked.

"No," I told him.

He then told me that it was a beautiful city by the Pacific Ocean with scenic mountains in the background. They were hiring firefighters, and he had some connections back there. I gave him my address and said thanks and rejoined my friends.

After a couple more days in Texas and a stopover in Nashville, we headed back home. When I arrived, to my surprise, there was an application for the Tacoma Fire Department in my mailbox. He was a man of his word. I filled it out and mailed it back.

I was making preparations for a flight to Tacoma for my test when Detroit called. I was being called back to work. It seems that the feds came through with some funds, and the city called a few of us back. I called and let Tacoma know that I wouldn't be coming and thanked them. Who's kidding who? I'm not going anywhere. I'm part of the D, and the D is part of me. Yes, the mountains and the Pacific sounded nice, but I still had the river and a street called Mount Elliott.

CHAPTER 11

1978

A couple of months after I was called back, I was detailed to Squad 4. It was a regular stop for me; it seemed that I was detailed there every other day. On a cold winter night, at around two, we responded to an overturned tanker truck at the Lodge and Ford Freeway interchange, the busiest interchange in the city. When we arrived, we found a double-bottom gas tanker rolled over with the cab flipped upside down on top of one of the pups. Gas was spilling out everywhere. The driver was trapped inside.

Double-bottom gasoline tankers were very controversial at the time. They were two tankers (pups) pulled by a semi-tractor. What made them controversial was their shape. They were short in length and very tall in height, making them unstable in turns. It seemed that every week, another double tanker was overturning. There was a movement to ban them. I knew this would help their cause.

We climbed onto the cab, and we could see the driver, who was still alive but trapped inside. There was a small area on top of the wrecked cab that a person could squeeze through. Being the skinniest person up there, I figured that I should climb in. I removed my fire coat and helmet and crawled inside. Lieutenant Van Sickle and the other two squad guys remained on top to assist me. Chief Byrum ordered everyone else back. They formed a perimeter back about thirty feet, and then they turned on handlines to fog to help prevent a fire. There are very few things in the world that are more dangerous than gasoline when you have thousands of gallons leaking. A spark in the right place could make things very interesting.

When I crawled through the opening, I found the driver trapped and in pain. His leg was broken and pinned underneath thousands of pounds of steal. We've all seen movies or heard tales where someone in this situation would tie a tourniquet, pull out a saw, cut off the leg, and everyone would get out okay. But this was reality. I would have to free his leg, the sooner, the better, because the only way I was leaving this unlit firecracker was with the driver, leg and all.

I had a Halligan bar, the Jaws of Life, and two very weak flashlights. To make matters worse, some of the water overspray was getting in and giving everything, including us, a slick, icy coating. I wished now that I had never taken off my warm rubber fire coat. But no matter how bad it was for me, it was way worse for the poor trapped driver with his smashed leg. We introduced ourselves. His name was Eddy. "Eddy," I said, "the more you scream, the more nervous I get, and the more nervous I get, the longer it's gonna take me to get us out of here."

Using the Jaws, I tried to lift some of the debris off his legs. I then tried to brace what I lifted with the Halligan bar and some wood blocks. There was so little room to maneuver, and I was worried that I could shift the weight the wrong way and it would all come down on us. The chief called for a heavy-duty tow rig, but you don't want to start lifting the upside-down cab with two men still inside. I kept working away, move a little here, move a little there. Eddy was doing better, hardly a whimper. In fact, I think I was whimpering more than he was.

Finally, after around thirty minutes of bending, lifting, moving, and some yelling, I freed his leg. "He's free!" I yelled. I pulled him up and over me as the squad guys reached in and pulled him out and placed him on a waiting stretcher. Then they reached in and pulled me out. I was soaking wet and freezing as I climbed down and put my coat back on.

Chief Byrum walked up and said, "Nice job." Then he said something else to the lieutenant that really surprised me. "Put Firefighter Dombrowski in for a citation!"

A citation, I couldn't believe it. For the last six years, I had been stretching line, climbing ladders, and running into burning buildings. Never once did I think that I would get a citation. Citations are big events in the Detroit Fire Department. To earn one, you must save somebody, and that doesn't happen very often. You would think that with all the fires we get in Detroit, firefighters would be getting them every day, but no, they do not.

Two guys could run into a burning building, looking for trapped persons; one guy goes right, the other turns left. The guy who turned left finds the victim and earns a citation; the person who went right earns nothing even though they both faced the same danger. It seems that some firefighters are always saving victims and some firefighters never do. Before that cold night, I never did.

One night, just a few days before Christmas, when I was still new on the job, we responded to an apartment fire. It was a three-story apartment on Trumble Street. The first two floors were fully engulfed with fire. The first arriving crews put a ladder up to the third story and went in, looking for victims. I climbed up to the open third-story window, and when I got there, a firefighter appeared and handed me a small child. He was around six years old, dressed in pajamas, and out cold. I gasped. It was the most beautiful sight I ever saw in my life, a Norman Rockwell painting that came to life.

I carried the little boy down the ladder to the waiting arms of the EMS, the emergency medical service, who rushed him to the hospital. That was the moment, the beautiful moment that I knew that being a Detroit firefighter was the greatest job in the world. It was a scene that I always visualized when I thought of fighting fires. The fireman who handed me the child, I think his name was Bob Lynn. After handing him to me, he went back into the heat and smoke to look for others. I believe he got a citation for that, and he certainly deserved one.

But today, it would be my turn. Pulling a driver out of an overturned tanker and winning a citation, all in one day, I couldn't ask for a better day than that.

Lieutenant Van Sickle wrote up my citation. He did an extra fine job, I might add. A couple of months later, I was called down to headquarters along with a couple other firefighters to receive our citations. I cleaned my uniform, shined my shoes, and got a haircut. The chief drove me down to the headquarters, and we went up to the third floor boardroom. It was an oak-paneled room with red carpeting and chandeliers. The room had the bygone splendor of a time when Detroit was the center of industry.

There were a couple dozen people, including the three of us who were getting awarded, in the room. The commissioner presented each of us with a certificate. Then a group of women from the Polish Women's Auxiliary gave each of us a twenty-five-dollar bond. One of the ladies from the group took me aside and said, "I'm glad someone with a Polish name was getting an award. It's been a while."

"I'm glad someone with a Polish name is getting an award too," I said. She laughed.

Then someone from the commissioner's office walked up and said, "Dombrowski, you get to go to the 100 Club." The commissioner had looked through all the citations they gave out that year and picked three firefighters for the 100 Club. I would be one of the three.

The 100 Club is a benevolent organization that provides for the widows and dependents of firemen and police officers who are killed in the line of duty. The Detroit 100 Club was formed in 1950 by a gentleman named Bill Packer. He was a successful automobile dealer.

A police officer was killed in the line of duty back in 1950, and his widow was destitute. Bill Packer found out and wanted to help. He got one hundred people together, who each contributed one hundred dollars, and they gave the money to the widow. Since then, every time a cop or fireman is killed in the line of duty, the 100 Club steps in and pays off much of their debt. Today, there are 100 Clubs throughout America; sometimes they're called Blue Coats. But the very first one was started by Bill Packer in Detroit in 1950.

The 100 Club has an annual dinner in which three fire fighters and three police officers who have been cited for performing some act of bravery are picked to come and receive an award. It is a first-class event that every firefighter hopes to go to someday. This year would be my year, my first of two.

We all met at Engine 55. A limousine picked us up and chauffeured us down to the Renaissance Center, where the banquet would be held. Our first stop was a place called the Renaissance Club, where the commissioner bought us all a drink. Then we went to the ballroom. Fantastic! They had a long hors d'oeuvre table with a life-sized ice carving of a policeman and a fireman on each end of the table.

We sat down for an amazing dinner. Afterward, they called us up to the stage one at a time and told the audience our story, what heroic deed we had performed to get here. We were each given a watch, a gold-trimmed Longines. This was the first nice watch I ever had. Of all six of us receiving awards, I was the most awestruck by one of the cops' story.

This Detroit cop with shoulder-length blond hair was working undercover in Narcotics. He met some people selling cocaine on the streets of Detroit and infiltrated their group. He got so high up in the organization that he was dealing with the heads of the gang in Columbia. When the bust finally happened, it involved the FBI, Interpol, and various police agencies all over the world. They performed the worldwide drug bust in Greenwich mean time to coordinate the different agencies. At the time, it was the world's biggest drug bust, all due to one Detroit cop.

Later that night, over a beer, I got a chance to talk with that cop.

"Aren't you afraid that these drug dealers are going to come looking for you?" I asked.

"No," he laughingly said, "these people know the chance they take when they deal drugs, and getting busted is part of it. They screwed up by letting me in, and now they're in jail. I'm the least of their thoughts. Besides, I think I feel a lot safer busting drug dealers than climbing into overturned tankers."

I guess that's it. Cops feel comfortable doing cop stuff, and we feel comfortable doing fire stuff. And all these movers and shakers of Detroit, the 100 Club members, who put on this wonderful night, feel comfortable doing what they do. It's nice to know that, when something happens, folks like this have our backs.

CHAPTER 12

Just before the 100 Club banquet, I met my gorgeous wife, Linda. I was at the First Edition Bar, playing foosball with a couple of other off-duty firemen. I noticed two girls who were playing pinball. They weren't regulars; they looked different than the usual girls who hung out there. They wore jeans and baggy sweaters and wore their hair carefree over their shoulders. They looked like a couple of college girls. I walked up and introduced myself.

"Hello, my name is Bob."

"Hello, my name is Linda," she said in the loveliest voice I ever heard. Then she flashed me her movie-star smile. That was it, love at first sight. We were married a year and a half later.

We bought a small house on the west side of Detroit on Bramel Street in a neighborhood called Copper Canyon because of all the city employees who live there. At the time, Detroit had a strict residency rule that required all employees of the city to live in the city.

It was also at this time that I first ventured into fire-department politics. There were two issues that I thought were unfair and needed to be changed. The first was the before-mentioned residency rule, which would become a huge future battle for me. The second had to do with our retirement pension.

At the time, Detroit police and firefighters had two pensions, the old system for everyone hired before 1969 and the new system for those of us hired after 1969. At the time, the old system was much better. They could retire with twenty-five years seniority, plus they had an escalator clause. That meant that every time the active firemen and cops got a pay raise, the retired firemen and cops would get the same pay raise. The new plan had no escalator, and you had to work until you were fifty-five years old and have had thirty-five years of service.

This was a huge issue in 1979. With inflation running in double digits, retiring with a fixed pension meant poverty in a short time. When we complained, the old guys had the same answer, "Well, if you young guys don't like it, then why don't you do something about it?" And do something about it we did.

Sitting around Engine 33's quarters between runs, another firefighter named Fabio and I planned our strategy. First, we had to organize the young guys, those of us hired in the last ten years. Second, we had to present a demand to the union to make improving the new pension a priority, next contract.

We researched and got all the information we could on pensions. We made up flyers and distributed them throughout the department. Next, we rented a hall and set a date for our first new pension meeting.

This movement of ours became a big hit with the young guys. Everybody was excited; guys all over the city were calling us, wanting to join in. We formed a steering committee and had meetings at my house, planning our strategy. About five of us were sitting around my kitchen table one afternoon when the phone rang. My wife answered it and said, "Bob, it's Earl Berry," and she handed me the phone.

We all stopped in our tracks. There was no bigger name in the Detroit Fire Department than Earl Berry, our legendary union president, and we knew he would be pissed off.

"Hello, Earl," I said.

"Dombrowski, what the heck are you doing?" he screamed. "Are you trying to start your own union. Are you trying to be another Mark Bigley?"

"Of course not," I said. "We're just having an information meeting about the new pension. Everyone is invited, including you."

"No way would I be there. That is what we have union meetings for!" And he hung up. True to his word, Earl didn't show up at the meeting, but most other elected union officials did.

The meetings were well run and thought provoking, a true learning experience for me. We had two in all, and they were well attended. Half of the guys were serious, wanting to learn all they could and fight for pension improvements. The other half made it a stop between bar stops, looking for a few laughs. We managed to organize our demands and present them to the union.

The next contract, the union succeeded in getting a twenty-five-year retirement for the new pension. They didn't get us an improvement in the escalator, but one out of two wasn't bad.

In 1979, Detroit purchased a brand-new fireboat. They named it the *Curtis Randolph* after the first black firefighter killed in the line of duty. *Curtis Randolph* was a new firefighter, a TFF or trial firefighter assigned to Engine 32, an east-side company. Two years earlier, on October 29, 1977, just two days before Devil's Night, he had stretched on a vacant dwelling on fire on Lillibridge Street. He was up in the attic, fighting the fire, when there was a back draft, and he was sadly killed.

The *Curtis Randolph* replaced the old boat called the *John Kendall*. The old boat was a 135-foot long steam-powered ship manned by a double crew consisting of the marine crew, five men to operate the boat, and another five firefighters to fight the fires.

The Curtis Randolph was seventy feet long and could pump eleven thousand gallons of water per minute. It would only have a crew of two boat operators and no firefighters. When needed, Central would dispatch a fire company to man the boat.

The fire company that Central would dispatch would usually come from the Seventh Battalion, my battalion. We ended up spending a lot of time down at the fireboat, going to school, learning how to operate the deck handlines, and operating the big water cannons.

Summertime was usually a busy time for the fireboat, with all the waterfront festivals and the annual boat races. If you were lucky, you could get detailed to the boat for one of the events and spend a hot summer day relaxing on the river rather than running into burning buildings. The best event of all was the fireworks.

Every summer, around the Fourth of July, Detroit puts on one of the biggest fireworks shows in the country. They have three sixty-foot barges loaded with three- and four-inch mortars and rockets that they tow out to the middle of the river. It was always my favorite detail. The fireboat was the closest boat to the barges. It was a great spot to watch the show. The first amazing thing that I noticed was how many rockets they launched. Literally thousands are launched in a thirty-minute time frame. They go straight up and explode right overhead, then ash falls on you like rain.

The Zembeli family from Pennsylvania, who were one of the best fireworks companies in America, put on the show. When we met with them beforehand to coordinate our operations, they told us what a great safety record they had.

"Okay," I jokingly said, "hold up your hands so we can see if you have all your fingers."

Zembeli held up his hand, and he was missing two fingers. Boy, was I ever embarrassed. "Don't worry," he said. "I lost these in 'Nam."

Damn, why did I say that?

You would think everyone in the city would have been happy having this $1.6 million piece of equipment, which the feds paid for, patrolling our waterfront, but you would be wrong. Mayor Young, who was always looking for extra money and looking for new ways to screw the fire department, decided to sell the fireboat and lay off the crew. This was inexplicable when you consider that Detroit has over twenty-five miles of water frontage, much of it high-rise and industrial. Detroit has had a fireboat since 1893, and the Detroit River is one of the busiest waterways in America.

Another city, I believe it was Boston, wanted to buy it. But there was a problem. The federal government had paid for the boat, and if Detroit wanted to sell it, Detroit couldn't keep the money. The money would all go back to the feds. So that ended that, and Detroit ended up keeping the fireboat. And it can still be seen today, proudly running up and down the beautiful Detroit River.

CHAPTER 13

1980

The year 1980 was a pivotal year for Detroit firefighters. It was the year we went from one of the highest paid fire departments in America to one of the lower paid departments for northern large cities. The previous eight years I was on the department, we enjoyed one of the highest wage scales in America, probably in the world. But all that came crashing down with the 1980 contract.

Contract-signing time was always a fun event. The union would rent the big Knights of Columbus hall on Larkin Street to hold the large crowd of members who would show up. President Earl Berry would then announce our new base wage, $15,000; $18,000; $21,000; $25,000; and on and on. Every couple of years, we would get a nice raise. Plus we had COLA, cost of living adjustments; whenever inflation went up, so did our paychecks.

President Berry, after announcing our new pay raise, would then announce "As of today, we are the highest paid fire department in America" to the cheers of the grateful membership. Those were the days.

We were one of the highest paid departments because we were one of the highest wage earning cities. Detroit is America's auto capital, and during the auto-boom years, 1940s through the 1970s, Detroit was a very rich area. If you couldn't get a job here, you were unemployable. The Big Three gave us high wages and a high standard of living.

Then everything changed. We got high gas prices and foreign imports. Detroit cars were having trouble selling, and if the Detroit car companies are having trouble, the city of Detroit is really in trouble.

In 1980, Detroit was facing bankruptcy. To save the city, the fire and police unions had to agree to wage concessions. We had to agree to a three-year pay freeze and give up COLA permanently. These were the years of double-digit inflation. It ended up being four years of no raises; our pay in real dollars fell by over one-third, and we never made up for it.

Believe it or not, that wasn't the worst part of the contract. Losing one-third of our wages was terrible but understandable; after all, the city was in a bind. What wasn't at all understandable was that the union also agreed to leave the seniority system off the contract and take it to a separate arbitration.

There is no more important issue to Detroit firefighters than our beloved seniority system. There was no more hated issue to Mayor Young than our seniority system. The seniority system gave us all an equal chance for promotion. The seniority system stopped Mayor Young, or any other mayor, from promoting their cronies. For the union to agree in a concession contract to leave this issue off, I think, was nothing short of criminal.

I personally thought that the whole union board should be thrown out of office. But the following election, they were all reelected, except for one director named John, who was the only person to vote against the contract. Go figure.

The year 1980 was also the year of the Republican National Convention in Detroit. July of 1980, Republicans from all over America came to our fair city to nominate Ronald Reagan to become our fortieth president. I guess it was ironic that President Reagan, the man who broke up the Aircraft Controllers Union, the start of the fall of unions in America, was nominated in what was then the biggest union town in America.

I don't know how happy God was about all this because right during the convention, on Wednesday, July 16, he turned the sky green and gave Detroit one of its worst storms in history.

I was detailed to Engine 48 that day, the slowest company in the city, and looked forward to an easy twenty-four hours. We ended up having thirty runs that day. That's a lot for the slowest engine in the city. The storm came in around 10:00 a.m. The sky suddenly turned dark green, and the wind and everything else came to an eerie standstill. Then the wind started to howl, and the rain came pouring down, and the alert started going off.

We jumped on the rig and headed into the storm. You couldn't see a thing. I'll bet we bumped into ten cars that morning; there was nothing you could do. Trees were falling down, power lines and transformers were falling all over with sparks shooting into the air. Roofs were blown off houses; drive-in movie screens were crashing to the ground. We went from run to run, putting out fires, mostly small fires, luckily, and cutting fallen tree limbs so folks could get out of their cars and houses. We also had a ton of downed electrical wires that we had to deal with.

One thing happened later that day that I will never forget. We received a run that a child had fallen down a sewer. When we arrived, there was an excited crowd around an open manhole cover. People were shouting and screaming, "A child fell down the sewer. You firemen got to get him!"

I walked up and looked down and thought, *Damn, this is bad.* The sewer went down about twenty feet, and at the bottom was rushing water that looked like the Colorado River. My boss told me that, because I was the youngest man, I would have to go down there and look for the kid. He pulled out our old rope, tied me up, and they started to lower me down when Ladder 13 pulled up.

Sergeant Hood jumped out of the truck and shouted, "What's going on?" We told him, and he said, "Does anybody know whose child fell down that sewer?" Nobody knew. He then said, "Nobody's going down in that sewer until we know for sure that there's a kid down there!" Well, it turned out no one had fallen in the sewer. It was just somebody thinking that they saw something that they never saw.

But what was more important was that he made a decision that may have saved my life. Never send someone into a dangerous situation unless you're sure you have to. This may seem so obvious, but it isn't, not when you're on the scene and people are shouting and screaming for you to do something. The British have a saying, "Those that can keep their heads when those all around our losing theirs."

That's why I'll always believe in our seniority system. Younger firefighters watching older, experienced firefighters and officers is the way we learn in Detroit. There are some things that textbooks can never teach you.

A couple months later, I was detailed to Engine 27, although there was no Engine 27. The city had removed it and replaced it with a lime-green pickup truck with a pump and some one-and-a-half-inch line that they called a Tac. Ladder 8 and Chief 7 also ran out of there. Around midnight, we were sitting, watching a rerun of a Roberto Durán fight on HBO, when the alert went off.

"Tac Truck and Chief, accident on the Ambassador Bridge," the guy on watch yelled.

I jumped behind the wheel and headed for the bridge. The Tac rode with three men: a driver and boss who sat inside the cab and a firefighter who rode on the back platform, holding on for dear life.

When we got to the scene, we found one car had rear-ended another car. Traffic was blocked in both directions, and people were outside their vehicles, milling around. Most of the crowd was teenagers who were returning to the States after drinking in Canada. Canadian law allowed people to drink at nineteen. This was a big hit with the Michigan youth.

We investigated the incident. There was no one trapped and no fire, and we were about to go back in service when one of the inebriated teens decided to shove the chief. Frank Garza saw this then ran full speed, tackled the kid, and began fighting with him. Then another teen jumped on Frank's back. Frank threw him off and began to also wallop him.

Now the first person that Frank tussled with got up off the ground, climbed up on the bridge railing, and announced to the world, "I'm jumping off."

We showed him no sympathy, and someone yelled, "You don't have the guts to jump." Then the bridge employees ran over, wrestled the guy off the railing, told us that they could handle it, and we could go. The show was over.

Frank Garza, who was one of the nicest human beings on the planet, was standing next to me, huffing and puffing, trying to catch his breath. I turned to him and asked, "What the heck was that all about?"

"I don't know, Bob. I guess it was watching that Duran fight that got me all geeked up."

We climbed back in the Tac and headed for home as I wondered what else was on HBO.

A few days later, I was detailed to Ladder 20 down in the Cass Corridor. On that day, there was a firefighter from Melvindale. Melvindale was a small suburb just south of Detroit. Suburbs around Detroit often send their younger firefighters to Detroit to gain some fire experience. This would be his second day riding with us, and I asked him how his first day was.

"Aw, you guys aren't so tough. Last day, we only had a couple of runs with one small fire. Once in Melvindale, we had a house fire and a garage fire both on the same day," he said.

"Maybe we'll have a busier day today," I said.

And busy we were. Between 8:00 p.m. and 6:00 a.m., we had seven working fires. They were all good ones, third-floor rears of apartment buildings and dwellings going throughout. Around 6:00 a.m., I walked by the kitchen and there he was, filthy dirty and totally exhausted. He was sipping a hot cup of coffee while staring off into space.

"Hey, why don't you go upstairs. You can still get an hour of sleep," I said.

"What for? It's not going to end. It's never going to end. How do you guys do it? How do you guys come here day after day and go to all these fires?" he asked.

"Well, it's like anything else. You get used to it. You really have to come and experience it for yourself like you did to understand what we go through," I told him.

Nobody fights as many fires as we do! We are the Detroit Fire Department, I thought to myself as I climbed the stairs, hoping to get an hour of sleep.

CHAPTER 14

In 1982, Detroit saw its first Grand Prix. How thrilling, a Formula 1 race right in the heart of downtown. Every day, the newspapers would report more exciting plans for the event, what downtown roads they would race on, where the race drivers would stay, and so on. Then one day, the paper reported that suburban firefighters would be working the race course, not Detroit's. "What!" I cried when I read that. "Suburban firefighters in Detroit at our big event? Nope, that's not happening."

I called the union to complain, but they had no idea what I was talking about. Then I searched (this was before computers) until I finally found the guy in charge of the Formula 1 firefighters (crash crew), who I'll call Lawrence. I told him that this was our town and a union town and if he needed firefighters protecting his race course, he'd better use us.

"No problem," Lawrence said. "If Detroit guys want the job, great. Of course, there is some training involved."

We agreed that I would get him a list of firefighters. I sent out a flyer and had thirty names right away. We had to go to two schools, one at Waterford Race Course, about an hour north of Detroit, and another at Marathon Refinery on the west side of the city.

School at the Waterford Race Course was a lot of fun. They had us there during an actual sports car race. We were taught how to safely go onto the race track and remove a driver from a wreck. European auto racing, unlike American auto racing, doesn't always stop for wrecks. You do not go on the track until it's safe, no matter how bad the wreck is. That's why they pay Formula 1 drivers the big bucks.

School at Marathon was just extinguishing fires with a bunch of different fire extinguishers, nothing that we hadn't performed a thousand times before.

After we had finished our schools and were in a group, listening to some final instructions from Lawrence, a firefighter whispered in my ear, "How much are we going to get paid?"

"I don't know," I whispered back. I raised my hand and spoke. "Lawrence, you never told us how much we will get paid."

"Paid? You guys are all volunteers. Nobody gets paid!"

Well, needless to say, the boys were not happy about this, and they all blamed me! But it all worked out, and we had a lot of fun working the three days. The city let us switch our workdays so we could be there. The race went well, and there were no major crashes.

A Detroit Police dive team member who was there told me a funny story. Part of the race course was on Atwater Street, which runs along the Detroit River, and they were worried about a race car falling into the river. They got an old, junk car and pushed it into the river as an experiment to see if they could retrieve it. The Detroit Police divers jumped in, and forty-five seconds later, they had recovered the car.

"Amazing," they all said, "forty-five seconds!" Nowhere in the world was any dive crew this fast. Everybody there was clearly impressed with the divers, but instead of leaving well enough alone, they decided to push the car in again. This time, the current, which is six miles an hour, took over. The cops jumped in, looked for the car, but couldn't find it. A couple of hours later, they called the search off.

One of the auto companies lent us a little red foam fire truck, and as the race came to an end that Sunday, a few of us firemen, along with a few DPD divers, decided to take it for a victory lap around the course. Along the way, someone pulled the lever that released the foam.

Coming down the course, we looked like a welcoming fireboat shooting its water spray, only it was gallons and gallons of foam.

Lawrence, who was in charge of safety, jumped in his official pace car and was chasing us. By now, his car was covered with foam so thick that he had to put his windshield wipers on. He would stick his head out of his driver's window, yelling at us to stop, while trying to dodge the airborne foam, but his timing wasn't real good.

Poor guy. All I keep seeing is his head covered in foam like some angry snowman and his wipers going back and forth, trying to keep up with the white onslaught. That's my last memory of the 1982 Detroit Grand Prix.

Detroit is a great sports town. We had the Tigers, Lions, Red Wings, Pistons, Wolverines, Spartans, and the DFD teams. Sports are also a big part of the department, although I never played on any of our teams. But running with them, you couldn't help but be a part of them.

The DFD hockey team has been around for as long as anyone can remember. They practiced at Joe Lewis Arena and, before that, at the Olympia Stadium, the same places that the Red Wings played. The Detroit Police and Fire hockey games were legendary and would bring huge crowds.

The DFD basketball team is mainly made up of former Division 1 and ex-pro basketball players who are now firemen. I used to take my son to watch them play at the old police gym. He thought he was watching the Pistons. Saved me a few bucks too. They were so good that, in the early nineties, they scrimmaged the Michigan Wolverines and beat them. This was the famous Fab Five Wolverines that played in two national championship games.

We always had a bunch of DFD baseball teams. There are fire department baseball tournaments all over America; Detroit would usually send one or two teams. It wasn't uncommon for a Detroit team to win the whole tournament.

Detroit firefighters used to put on their own baseball tournament. They started out on Belle Isle, a downtown island park, and then they moved to outer areas of town. It was a wonderful three-day affair, attracting firefighters from all over America. The Burn Center Tournament, it was called, ended on Sundays with a celebrity softball game. Local celebrities showed up in scores. All told, they raised thousands of dollars for the Detroit Medical Burn Center.

It was during one of our Burn Center Tournaments, with hundreds of out-of-town firefighters in town, that we had a real famous fire. The Buhl Building fire, as it was called, happened on June 13, 1982. The Buhl Building is an old skyscraper in the heart of downtown. A lot of law offices were located in the building, and on the eighth floor were the offices of the Bell and Hudson Law Firm.

That June morning, a guy named Robert Harrington went there to collect $2,500 that attorney Ed Bell owed him. Under his coat, he hid a shotgun and a bottle of gasoline. When the young receptionist told him that she didn't have his check, he pulled out his shotgun and shot her dead. He then ran through the offices, shooting at everyone he saw, pouring gasoline everywhere, and lighting it.

The people in the offices ran for the windows. When Ladder 1, the first truck on the scene, pulled up, they saw that the eighth floor was on fire, and people were hanging out of the windows, getting ready to jump.

Ladder 1 immediately raised their one-hundred-foot aerial, but it was too short. It couldn't reach the eighth floor. People started jumping. Then they carried a twenty-foot straight-beam ladder up to the top of the one-hundred-foot aerial, spliced it into the top of the aerial, climbed up, and began rescuing trapped victims. They also brought up a fifty-foot extension ladder, put it on a parapet, and began rescuing victims. It turned out to be one of the great high-rise rescues in modern history.

Eve August was the receptionist he killed. Two people died jumping out the windows, and thirty-eight others were injured. It's unclear how many were rescued and how many lives were saved by the DFD that June morning, maybe hundreds.

A couple of days later, I was on duty, and we were discussing the Buhl fire. My lieutenant at the time was also a part-time fire instructor for Michigan State University. He always said that Detroit didn't have enough training.

So I asked him, "What did you think of that rescue, Lieutenant?"

"Dumb luck," he said.

No, you're wrong. It was smart luck.

CHAPTER 15

Devil's Night is what Detroit firefighters are well-known for throughout the world. It's the name given to October 30, the night before Halloween. Reporters, professors, tourists, and firefighters from all over the world come to Detroit to watch the strange phenomenon of dwellings, storefronts, garages, apartment buildings, and vacant factories burn to the ground in an orgy of lawlessness and arson.

Detroit, with its huge Catholic population, was one of the first cities in America to celebrate Halloween or All Hallows' Eve. November 1 is a Catholic holy day called All Saints' Day. Back in medieval Europe, on October 31, the night before All Saints' Day, poor people would go door-to-door, shouting, "Help the poor!" People would give them food with the understanding that they would go to church the next morning and pray for their dead relatives. Catholic Europeans brought the tradition to America, where it became Halloween.

And right from the beginning, the night before All Hallows' Eve became a day of mischief. Back in the twenties and thirties and forties and fifties, kids would go out and ring doorbells, soap windows, and kick over trash cans. The night became known as Devil's Night.

Back in 1972, when I first started the department, Devil's Night consisted mainly of pulled fire alarm boxes, dumpster fires, and an occasional garage fire. We were kept busy all night with small stuff. But that began to change in the late seventies. Box pulling and dumpsters were replaced with dwelling fires, store fires, you name it.

Devil's Night became our busiest night. We would run all night, going from fire to fire, but nobody but us seemed to know about it. All that changed in the early eighties, when the media began to take notice. Suddenly, that was all anybody talked about. We were the top news story and not just local news. CNN, ABC, even networks from countries as far away as Japan sent news crews. Our arsonists had made us famous. Devils Night became the Super Bowl of American firefighting!

When I visited New York, I stopped in their FDNY store. There you could purchase T-shirts from all their different fire stations. They only had two non–New York T-shirts for sale: Boston and Detroit's Devil's Night T-shirts.

As the media took notice, so did the city. Devil's Night now consisted of a three-day period—Devil's Night, Halloween, and the day after, just for good measure. The city set a dusk-to-dawn curfew and set up a night court to handle offenders.

The city would organize the department into command posts. Of the forty-five fire stations we had at the time, they would close down thirty-five and crowd us into the ten fire stations or command posts.

We hated this; over three hundred of us crowded into just ten fire stations with few places to sit or relax. We usually stood around, waiting for our next run, watching HBO that the cable company provided free for the night, eating hot dogs provided by the Fireman's Fund, eager for the next fire just to get out of there.

The city makes every employee, from garbage men to typists, work, all paid overtime, of course. In fact, the only city employees working Devil's Night for no overtime pay are the firefighters. They just cancel our furloughs and days off and make us come in.

Cops from all over Southeast Michigan are brought in. Added to this are five thousand volunteers. They ride up and down the streets all night with yellow flashers on top of their cars. Despite all this, the fires kept coming. The highest was 810 fires in 1984.

Devil's Night, if not for the tragedy of all the destruction to our city, was an exciting night for us, kind of like soldiers going into combat. They had plenty of guys working due to canceling the days off; we would ride with four or five on a rig, as opposed to the norm of three. You would respond from fire to fire, all over the city.

East side, west side, north side, it didn't matter. With all the fires, you just went. When you pulled up, you would be greeted by scores of people in their vehicles with the flashing yellow lights. Reporters from all over the world would be on the scene, speaking in French or Japanese and taking hundreds of pictures. Civilians would bring you pop, water, and treats. You felt like a celebrity.

Yet there would still be the fires, hundreds of them, and usually, by the time you got there, they would be burning out of control. One dwelling would turn into two or three. One apartment unit on fire would advance to a second alarm with the whole building going.

One year, I was running out of the Seventh Battalion command post in Southwest Detroit. We had two doctoral students from the Massachusetts Institute of Technology working on their doctorate degrees. They were studying conflagrations. A conflagration is when a fire gets so big it creates its own oxygen then sometimes burns down the whole city, such as the Great Chicago Fire.

They told me that on Devil's Night, Detroit would be perfect for a conflagration with all the fires and the old wooden dwellings built so close together. They rode the rigs all night and saw plenty of fires and afterward said, "Detroit would never have a conflagration for one reason, the incredible speed that the DFD puts fires out." They traveled all over America and observed firefighters in action in many places and said, "Nobody puts out fires quicker than Detroit." That's the DFD.

The morning after Devil's Night, no matter how tired we were, we always met up at a fireman's bar to discuss the events of the evening. Reporters were always there, asking us how many fires we had. The city usually gave them questionable figures, trying to make things look better than they were, and they wanted to double-check them with us. We then headed home for some badly needed sleep, knowing that tomorrow morning we would be back and doing it again.

Over the years the city managed to get the situation under control. It took a combined effort of the fire department, all the surrounding police departments, the media, and thousands of volunteers. They even changed the name to Angel's Night. We still get a lot of fires on those nights but nothing like the 1980s or the 1990s. Hopefully it stays that way.

CHAPTER 16

1984

Detroit firefighters are big sports fans. Tigers, Red Wings, Pistons, Lions, we love them all. But unlike the civilian population, we don't always hope that they win the championship because it's bad for us. Detroiters usually like to celebrate by rioting and burning things.

In 1984, the Detroit Tigers won the World Series for the first time since 1968. The City went nuts, burning police cars and taxi cabs, smashing windows, and doing general mayhem. The next day, America woke up to stories of the pandemonium in Detroit. A famous photo of a Tiger fan named Bubba Helms standing in front of a burning Detroit Police car, holding a Tiger pennant, graced many newspaper's front page in America.

But we do like to bet T-shirts with other departments when one of our teams makes the playoffs. Whatever city our City was playing, we called the fire station that had the same engine company number as ours and bet usually thirty-six T-shirts.

Spring of 1984, the Pistons made the playoffs and would be playing the New York Knicks. We called Engine 33 in New York and bet thirty-six T-shirts and lost. We weren't worried because we already had the thirty-six T-shirts in the station basement.

An engine house project we had started earlier in the year at Engine 33 was making up T-shirts. We had a clever silk screen made up, or so we thought. The movie *Ghostbusters* was a big hit that year, and we had a silk screen made of the ghost from *Ghostbusters* wearing a fire helmet with Engine 33 on it with the words "Who you gonna call."

Silk-screening, like everything else, is an art that can be a little tricky to perfect. Many of our T-shirts were less than perfect, and we were having a tough time selling them to the other firemen. So when we lost a bet, we had plenty of unsold T-shirts, so we sent Engine 33 in New York thirty-six *Ghostbusters* T-shirts. They were not very happy with our shirts and sent us a thank-you note written on toilet paper.

Later that year, in October, came the big one, the Tigers in the World Series against the San Diego Padres. How exciting! The whole town had Tiger fever. We called Engine 33 in San Diego and bet thirty-six T-shirts.

This bet became big news in San Diego. The media in San Diego picked up the story of the fire-station bet with Detroit and called us up. The guys put me on the phone. It was a San Diego radio station, and we were live on the air. The DJ and I ribbed each other over who was the better team and who would win.

When the call was over, the phone rang again, and it was a San Diego TV station, and they asked if they could come to our Detroit station and interview me when they came to town. "Hell yes," I said and gave them the directions to Engine 33.

Engine 33 is located in Southwest Detroit, a place that has always been a tough area, even back when the City was great. Southwest Detroit is filled with polluting factories and steel mills. The color of the sky goes from light red to dark red. Across the street from Engine 33 was a line of vacant, dilapidated storefronts. Within one block in any direction were more burnt-out dwellings than in all of San Diego. The engine house itself was old and in disrepair with two worn-out, rusted fire trucks sitting inside.

San Diego, if you have ever been there, is the exact opposite of Detroit. I spent a little time there with the Navy and loved it. San Diego has the ocean, palm trees, beautiful weather, beautiful streets, filled with beautiful cars, driven by beautiful people. Even the navy chow hall served beautiful food.

The day that the San Diego TV station showed up for the interview, I wasn't there. The reporter asked for another volunteer, and a firefighter named Joe volunteered. They went out front and asked Joe a bunch of questions that Joe answered well. Then at the end, the reporter asked one last question.

"Joe," he asked, "When you think of San Diego, what word comes into your mind?"

Joe stopped for a second, looked up at the sky, then looked at the reporter and said, "Pollution."

Yes, everyone was a little surprised at Joe's view of San Diego. When asked about it later, Joe said, "I don't know. It was the first word that came to mind."

But the important thing was that Detroit won the World Series. Sure, we had the riot and mayhem that the world expects of Detroit, but it was still good to win for a change. And we got our shirts; SDFD Engine 33 sent us thirty-six T-shirts. They were thirty-six beautiful, professionally made T-shirts, not something that they made in their basement. I never expected anything less. Sorry, New York.

As all firemen do, I worked part-time jobs or leave-day jobs, as we called them, whenever we needed some extra money, which was always. I did everything from driving a truck to painting houses.

I worked for a moving company. Cross-country drivers would pull into town and would need a helper to load or unload the furniture; they would pay cash at one hundred dollars per day. Not bad money in the eighties. I also worked for various insurance companies, inspecting homes.

One day, I was driving a truck for a company called Allied Trucking. They would have us fill in for the regulars. I pulled into the alley behind the address I was delivering to, got out of the truck, and began knocking on the back door.

A minute later, two guys opened the door and excitedly said, "Sorry we took so long. Are you okay?"

"Sure, I'm okay. Why do you ask?" I asked.

Then they explained to me that the regular driver that I was filling in for was robbed and shoot the day before right where I was standing.

I looked down, and I could still see the dried blood. I thought, *How horrible. I have to quit this crazy job. Firefighting is dangerous enough.*

My biggest leave-day job was staying home and watching my kids. My wife, Linda, was an X-ray technician who worked part time on my days off. She was on the other unit, so to speak. She would take my work schedule to her doctor, and he would always let her work around it.

I would rush home every morning after being up all night fighting fires. There, I would usually lie on the couch as my three little sons ran wild throughout the house. I would try not to doze off, but it was hard not to. Suddenly, I would wake up after dozing off and panic! *Where are the kids! I don't hear the kids!* I'd find them. Somehow they were always all right, and somehow we all made it. And it was a lot more rewarding than driving that truck.

CHAPTER 17

1985

The year 1985 was a big year for me. It was the year that I became an elected union official. I was elected Seventh Battalion union director. There was an opening because the old Seventh Battalion director moved up to the executive board. It was the first of four times that I would run and get elected.

It was no surprise to most that I ran and that I won. I was always active in the union and rarely missed a meeting. From my first union meeting back in 1972, when the young guys made a motion that the union fight to change the haircut code, to the layoffs when we were protesting fire station closings, I was usually in the forefront as union activist.

Now in my thirteenth year on the job, I was an elected union official. I hit the ground running. I read the contract cover to cover. I attended every meeting and seminar I could. I made my rounds (visits to the battalion fire stations) faithfully, and I tried to write an informative monthly article. Sometimes it would be a little controversial.

Through some contacts I had, I found out that all our air compressors were broke. We had no way of filling our air tanks. The city was forced to secretly load up a truck full of air bottles and go to a northern suburb to fill them up. I wrote about this in my article, and the commissioner read it. He had no idea this was going on. My old classmate Bigley was his aide and got in big trouble over this discovery. I was making enemies fast.

Highland Park, a suburb completely surrounded by Detroit, decided to fire their entire fire department and convert to public safety officers (PSO). To do this, they had to hire part-time firefighters to cover their City until the PSOs were trained. The head of the Highland Park Firefighters Union brought us the list of part-time firefighters that they had hired. They were all Detroit firefighters.

This was a violation of everything unions stand for. You take an oath never to harm a union brother, and this group of Detroit firefighters was helping Highland Park to get rid of their entire fire department. They must be stopped, maybe even kicked out of the union.

But there was a problem. The guys that took the jobs in Highland Park were members of Phoenix, the association of black firefighters. Now this involved race, and in Detroit, whenever you involve race, it gets ugly, and back then, everything involved race. Phoenix got involved in the fight and scared most of the union officials off.

The union didn't want to confront the issue. I was pissed off. If our union does nothing to stop this, I thought, then I will go to the State Firefighters Union, and if they do nothing, then I will go to the International Association of Fire Fighters (IAFF) in Washington, but I will not stop until somebody stops these firefighters from taking those jobs. In the end, they all agreed and resigned their part-time jobs in Highland Park. I won, but I was getting a reputation.

We had a residency rule in Detroit. You had to live in the city or you would be fired. The City strongly enforced this rule. On one day alone, they fired thirty-four firefighters. The union got most of the guys their jobs back, but the issue was very controversial at the time. Most of the white guys thought we should be able to live outside the City, but most of the black guys didn't.

Shortly after I was elected, a firefighter who I'll call Jimmy got fired for residency violation. He had a home with a wife and kids in the suburbs; he also was the Medal of Valor winner, an award given to the Detroit firefighter who performs the most heroic save of the year. Jimmy ran into a burning house and saved five kids. They fired him anyway.

I went to court with him a couple of times and followed his case closely. In the end, they fired him, and he never got his job back. I was stunned and thought this should never happen. That's when I decided I would do something about it.

I was reading a publication that the Milwaukie Firefighters Union sent us and read that they had introduced a bill in the *Wisconsin* legislature to eliminate residency. I called them up, and they sent me a copy of the bill. When the bill arrived in the mail, I got some Wite-Out and covered the word Wisconsin and typed in *Michigan*. Then I made a copy of the bill on our copy machine. When finished, it looked like our own lawyers had made it.

My next move was to get the State Firefighters Union to get this bill to Lansing. Jerry, another union director who was just as passionate about eliminating residency as I was, was elected to attend the state convention that year and agreed to submit the bill to the legislative committee. Jerry went to the convention, submitted the bill, and returned the conquering hero. We were all set, or so we thought.

A few months passed, and I heard nothing. Another firefighter who knew what I was doing told me that his wife worked in Lansing for a lobbyist, and nothing had been done on our bill. I called her up, and she explained to me how bills were introduced in the state legislature, and once they're introduced, they get a number. No number, no bill.

A short time after, the state union was holding their annual legislative conference. I went and sat there and listened as our state union president told us of all the magnificent things they were doing in Lansing on all the issues we wanted, including residency. When he finished, I raised my hand to be recognized, got up, and went to the microphone.

"Mr. President," I said, "with all due respect, every word out of your mouth about residency was bullshit."

The entire conference went wild; the union president banged his mallet and yelled that I was out of order. People shouted and roared as I explained all the intricacies I had learned about their inaction concerning our bill. The lawyer got up, grabbed the mike, and began to explain all the difficulties that this bill would cause.

"That's just perfect," I yelled. "Not only didn't they do anything about residency, our own lawyer tells us they're never going to do anything!" The crowd was on my side.

I went back to my seat. Then someone opened the exit door and called me out into the hallway. When I got there, there was our president, screaming and threatening me.

"How dare you come here and insult me! I should punch you in the face!" Two guys were holding him back from attacking me.

"I got nothing to say to you," I said then turned to leave.

Just then, a person who I had never seen before stepped up, grabbed my arm, and said, "Wait, I'd like to talk to you."

He introduced himself and told me that he was our lobbyist in Lansing.

"If you're going to tell me that he wasn't lying through his hat to me, then I'm outta here," I said.

"No, of course he was lying," he said with a laugh. "I'm surprised that you knew that."

Then he explained to me that the state union gave him a list of legislative actions they wanted him to work on, some more important than others, and this was on the very bottom of the list.

"We didn't think residency was that big of an issue with you guys," he said.

Then he asked me if I could give him a month. "Sure," I said. "What do I have to lose? I've waited thirteen years for this."

And true to his word he was, because one month later, our lobbyist, who I will call Darrel, called and said, "Get a pen and paper. I've got some numbers for you." He gave me a bill number and a name of the state representative, Debbie Stabinaw (a Michigan senator at the time of this writing), who would introduce the bill.

You cannot imagine how happy I was that day. It is very hard for an American, as I am, as you are, to live in this country but not be able to enjoy one of its greatest freedoms—the freedom to choose where you live. I gave that freedom up when I became a fireman. It was unfair, I thought. My wife gave it up when she married me, also unfair. Getting that bill number was one of the monumental days of my life.

Winston Churchill said at the end of the Battle of Britton, "This is not the end, but perhaps the end of the beginning." Those words best describe that moment when our bill was first introduced. It would be fourteen years before the bill would be signed into law, fourteen years of one of the greatest battles this union or any fire union would ever fight. That was a fourteen-year fight that would come very close to costing me my job and my sanity.

Another concern we were forced to deal with in my first year as a director was the City's attempt to change the seniority system—our holy grail, our sacred promotional system. As I wrote earlier, in 1980 the union and the City agreed to take one issue into arbitration: the seniority system. It took four years for a decision, but in 1984 the arbitrator ruled in our favor.

The City appealed the arbitrator's decision. No problem, we thought, it's an open-and-shut case. The union followed the law, won fair and square in arbitration, and the city had no case. The City went in front of a judge named Helene White. But instead of her just throwing the case out as we had expected, she said she was going to review it and then, to our shock, make a decision on our seniority system.

After a whole year of reviewing it, she notified us that she was ready with her decision. We were a new union board, and we were the ones to have to deal with this event that could be devastating to our membership.

When we got to her courtroom, it was packed; every city official you could think of, short of Coleman Young, was there. My old classmate Bigley was there with his Cheshire-cat smile. Clearly they must have gotten the word that they had won, we assumed. We took our seats in the back and waited for the end of the world as we knew it.

When Judge White came in, a surprisingly nice-looking lady, she said she had a couple of small cases to attend to before she got to the big one! Oh boy, we're screwed. After what seemed to be hours, it was our turn.

Judge White started out by telling us about herself. She said that when she was first handed this case, she couldn't believe it—in this day and age, a promotional system based entirely on seniority, a system where a bunch of old white guys are officers just because they got hired first, few black and no women officers. Bigley and the rest of the City officials could hardly contain themselves.

But she said, before she changed anything, she wanted to learn everything about it. She said the union had a great lawyer, Ted Sachs, one of the best labor lawyers in the country, and he would certainly appeal her decision. That's why it took her so long. Then she said a funny thing happened. The more she learned about the seniority system, the more it made sense to her. The City side looked shocked. Bigley almost fell out of his chair.

She then spent the next hour going step-by-step over every part of the seniority system to our incredible delight and to the City's incredible disappointment.

"Everyone who stays in the firefighting division will eventually get promoted: white, black, male, female. And they will be promoted the same way and time the older white men were promoted. How could that not be fair?

"Experience is the most important factor in firefighting, I learned, and what system offers a more experienced officer core than Detroit. You want to promote lieutenants in fire prevention who haven't fought fires in years to captains in firefighting? How could that be fair or good?" Judge White went on and on like this, at times almost scolding the City for their inane proposal.

Afterward, we all headed to Casey's Bar for a couple of well-deserved cold ones and let the boys know the great news. Yes, right will win out over wrong. You just have to keep the faith and get a good judge who does her homework.

CHAPTER 18

On a cold, snow-covered January night, we were responding engine alone to a still alarm. When we pulled up, we saw that we had a two-story dwelling with the lower level going pretty good. I jumped off the back end and was running to the back of the rig for the bundles when I heard people shouting from the roof. It was hard to see them through the smoke. Two people had crawled out through a dormer window and were shouting for help.

I dropped the bundle, grabbed a ladder, threw it up to the roof, and began to climb up to help them down. I was just stepping onto the second-story overhang when the ladder slipped out from under me, and down I went. I landed on my back with my air tank hitting the sidewalk first. Damn, I thought I broke my back. But I could move my hands and feet, so except for the pain, I'd be okay.

Other companies began arriving. They got the people off the roof, stretched the line, and began attacking the fire as I lay there on the sidewalk. The squad pulled up and ran up to me to see if I was all right.

The lieutenant asked, "Do you want to go to the hospital?"

"No, Lieutenant," I said, "it's a lovely night. I think I'll just lay here and look at the stars."

They loaded me up in the rig and hauled me to Detroit Receiving, where firemen get the best care in the world. As they dropped me off, one of the squad guys named Tawny said he would drop my fire gear off at my house on his way home.

The next morning, my wife was up, getting the kids ready for school, when she happened to look out the window and see Tawny throwing my fire gear over the fence.

"Hey, what are you doing?" she yelled out.

"Oh hi," Tawny said, "Bob asked me to drop his gear off."

"Okay, but where's Bob?"

"He's in the hospital. He fell off a roof last night and landed on his head. Don't worry, he's okay," Tawny shouted out as he pulled away.

My wife ended up calling the hospital to see if I was all right. The life of the wife of a Detroit firefighter can be tough at times.

The area where that fire happened was in Southwest Detroit, the Seventh Battalion; back in the 1980s, it was the busiest area in the City. To this day, it's still busy. Now the whole City is busy.

The majority of our fires, over 90 percent, are arson fires. No city in America has an arson problem close to Detroit's. We have individual arsonists in Detroit who are responsible for hundreds of fires. The arson squad arrests them; sometimes they go to jail. When they get out, it's back to setting fires.

The arsonists' names, especially the good ones, become well-known to us. One of the most famous arsonists families in Detroit is the Jacksons. Together they have started over three hundred fires. Dwellings, garages, stores, autos—you name it and they burned it. Their name strikes fear in people throughout Southwest Detroit.

The Jackson's lived in Southwest Detroit on a street where every house was gone, burned to the ground. The only houses left on the street were the Jackson's, and their next-door neighbor's.

Late one night, we got a box alarm. The house on fire was the one next door to the Jacksons. It was going throughout. It was a windy night, and the wind was blowing the fire toward the Jackson's house. In Southwest Detroit, most of the houses are only three feet apart. When we pulled up, the flames were starting to spread to the Jackson's house.

It would not be a good night for the Jackson family. We had all kinds of problems; we had a bad hydrant, and the engine couldn't get water. No matter how fast we worked, the fire grew, and before you knew it, the Jackson's' house was up in flames.

Poor Jackson's. Their house was burning to the ground and, with it, their furniture, their clothes, their pictures, and all their cherished possessions. This was just like so many other homes in Southwest Detroit, only this time, the Jackson's were on the receiving end. And they were not happy.

After the fire, I had to get the information for the fire report. I was questioning a young lady from the home, and when I asked her name, she gave me a different name from Jackson. I stopped and looked at her and said, "I thought your name was Jackson?"

She turned and ran off. She came back moments later with the entire Jackson clan, pointing her finger and shouting at me.

"You said we were the Jackson's. You knew that we were, and you firemen let our house burn down!"

Pretty shrewd, I thought. But I knew she was a Jackson and that she gave me a phony name because she had introduced herself to me a few months back at another fire. She even offered me a cigarette. I told her I didn't smoke.

I was surrounded by a hostile group of Jackson's, whose house had just burned down, and they were sure we let it happen. I felt like a lost tourist who had violated a No Trespassing sign in the Appalachian Mountains, but I was in good old Southwest Detroit. I had to think fast.

"Why did you ask if we were the Jackson's?" she screamed.

"Because the people down the street told me that that was your name. Why should the name Jackson mean anything to me?" I cleverly countered.

By then, the boys, who must have seen I was having a little trouble, joined me. It was a standoff until the police showed up, and then the Jackson's walked away. But it wasn't over. The next day, the whole Jackson clan went downtown to the commissioner's office, yelling and screaming that we let their house burn down.

The commissioner ended up throwing them all out of his office. Then they got a lawyer and tried to sue, but it didn't do any good. It was hard to prove that the fire department was malfeasant, almost as hard as proving arson. You would think that the Jackson's would know that.

38 YEARS

CHAPTER 19

Most of the Detroit fire stations are very old and in bad shape. Actually, every fire station in Detroit, new or old, is in bad shape. Many were built around the turn of the century. Every year, it seems, some fire station would reach its one-hundredth-year anniversary. The guys usually throw an engine house one-hundredth-year centennial party, invite the old guys who used to run there, and print up T-shirts with sayings like "Engine 10, 100 years of faithful service."

This is all part of the esprit de corps that Detroit firemen have. The old barns we run out of would fall apart if not for the loving care firemen put into them. Most fire stations have remodeling projects that firemen completed and paid for out of their own pockets.

It seems like every fire station has a patio out back, usually with an awning over it, a pond with coy, and a lovely garden. Inside they have updated kitchens, dining rooms with custom-made tables, painted and updated TV rooms, and sleeping dorms with private rooms—all this paid for and worked on by firemen.

A firefighter I knew left Detroit after ten years and got a job as a firefighter in a suburb in Oakland County. He told me a story about his new department reupholstering their La-Z-Boy recliners that they had bought for the firemen. When the La-Z-Boys returned, they were not comfortable enough, so they complained to their union. "These guys would have a tough time in Detroit," he jokingly told me.

Back in the early 1980s, I was running at Ladder 13 on the corner of Lafayette and Lawndale. The windows were the original single-pane wood windows, and they leaked badly. In the winter, we put plastic over them, but the wind would blow the plastic off. Snow would come right through, covering us as we tried to sleep. We would have to move our beds away from the windows just to keep the snow off us.

The City does supply fire stations with mattresses and box springs and bed frames, typically the cheapest ones available. They issue everyone a feather pillow, two wool blankets, one new sheet, and one pillowcase. You get a new sheet and pillowcase every year and a blanket and pillow every ten to fifteen years. You do need the wool blankets in the winter.

When fall came and the thermometer dropped and firemen turned on the furnaces for the first time, half of them wouldn't come on. The city would eventually send out some heat contractor to get the furnaces working. This could take a week or two. The only option they gave us was to run out of another station that had heat. There usually weren't enough beds or rooms at other stations, so you ended up staying and freezing.

Summer was a little better because we had air-conditioning in the dorms. We would take a collection and buy a big window AC unit that would cool the whole dorm. Downstairs was another story. We would block off the dining room with plastic sheets and install an AC unit. We couldn't cool the kitchen or the apparatus room. They just stayed hot.

To cool off the downstairs, we would open the apparatus doors, and then the kitchen would fill up with flies. We would put up flypaper and even put bug zappers in the kitchen, anything to get rid of those nasty flies, and it would get nasty.

The basements were another story. Whenever it would rain real hard, they would fill up with water and raw sewage. We would call the City, they would send out a plumber to get the water out, and then we would have to go down and clean it. I'm sure there is some Occupational Safety and Health Administration rule against this, but we did it anyway.

A big advancement the department made in the eighties was switching to computers for our runs. Part of the reason was that all our other systems broke. The Gamewell telegraph system we had when I started was a hundred years old and simply fell apart. The City phone lines were fifty years old and no longer worked. We were receiving our runs by radio, the only thing still working.

It was great getting these new computers. The runs would come over the computer, and we would get them on the printer. The only problem was they weren't hooked up to any alert system, so we improvised. We would leave an empty pop can on top of the printer, and when a run came, it would move the paper, causing the pop can to fall on the floor. We would hear the pop can hit the floor, and we would know that we would have a run.

Although we were advancing in computers, one area that we weren't advancing in was in our firefighting gear. Most departments were switching to the new-style gear, shorter coats and bunker pants. We were still wearing the long coats and the pull-up boots that went up to midthigh.

As a new union director, I made improving our firefighting gear one of my main issues. The city was against this because it would cost a lot of money to outfit the entire department with new bunker gear. I wrote complaints to the Michigan Occupational Safety and Health Administration, and I tried to change the state regulations to mandate bunker gear for all firefighters. But this would cost departments all over Michigan money, so that made it a nonstarter.

MIOSHA did eventually come to Detroit to investigate my complaint. The day the MIOSHA investigator came to town to inspect, we had six firefighters off duty with upper-thigh burns. Unbelievable. It was bad luck for the city, but amazingly, MIOSHA still didn't change the rule.

The next contract the union took the issue to arbitration. Ted Sachs even had me testify in arbitration on the need for bunker gear. In the end, we won, and the City was forced to equip us with new, modern bunker gear, which consisted of shorter coats and fire pants and short boots. It was a great victory for our union; it saved a lot of firemen a lot of injuries.

CHAPTER 20

1987

The date March 12, 1987, was a horrible day for Detroit firefighters. It was the day three Detroit firefighters were killed in the line of duty. In my thirty-eight-year career, fourteen Detroit firefighters died in the line of duty. But this was the only time in my career that we had three firefighters killed on the same day.

I was home, off duty, when a friend of my wife called and said, "Bob, I just heard on the radio that a Detroit firefighter was killed." I stopped what I was doing and called Engine 10. A voice answered and said yes, it was Lieutenant Schimek from here.

It was hard to believe that it was our own Lieutenant Paul Schimek who was killed. I jumped in my car and headed for Engine 10's quarters. As I sped down Michigan Avenue, I saw a department command car all lit up pass by in the other direction. It was Bigley. He must be going to Greenfield Village, where Paul's wife, Karen, worked, I thought. When I got to Engine 10, every off-duty firefighter was there or on their way.

Paul was a real pro, the kind of firefighter who always seemed to know the right answers, always doing the extra. He was a former union director who I often went to with questions. It was hard for us to believe that he got killed. Plus Paul was a lieutenant. Firefighters, not officers, generally were the ones who died in the line of duty. It just didn't make sense to us.

The fire was about a mile and a half away, a vacant three-story brick warehouse whose last tenant was the Ace Cloth Company, a rag company. In fact, Paul had taken Engine 10 there just a couple of days earlier and pre-fire-planned the building. Pre-fire planning is when firefighters walk through a building, assessing all the risks and dangers, then develop a plan on how we should fight a fire in there. Paul was always doing stuff like that.

A cruel twist of irony was his pre-fire planning might have helped lead to his death. The vacant warehouse was littered with debris, so much so that it was very hard to find the stairwells. Paul's pre-fire planning found the hidden stairwells and made note of them in the event of fire.

On that day, when box 382 came in, Paul and the crew knew the location well. When they pulled up, Paul saw smoke coming out of the third-floor windows. Paul had two firefighters on the back end. He told one to stay there and wait; they would drop him a rope for the one-and-a-half-inch line. Then Paul ran in, all the arriving firemen following him.

Paul, knowing right where the stairway was, found it then ran up to the third floor. When he got there, he found a pile of rags burning in the center of the room. Paul went to the empty window and lowered the rope for the one-and-a-half-inch line. Then all hell broke loose. The fire flashed, and the whole floor lit up. Paul and everyone else jumped onto the windowsills and hoped for rescue.

The skeleton crew below grabbed a forty-foot ladder and began rescuing the men as fast as they could. The flames grew too tough for a waiting Paul and blew him out. He fell to the ground, where he died upon impact. Another firefighter, Derrick Grochowski, was also blown out the window. He amazingly landed on the pole-to-pole electric wires and bounced in the air before hitting the ground and only suffered a broken collarbone.

We were still back at Engine 10's quarters with the TV on, sharing our grief. The fire was now a fifth alarm, the biggest you can have in Detroit. The news was making periodic announcements on the fire when they announced that two more firefighters may have been killed.

"What nonsense," we all said. "That's impossible. What the heck is wrong with the media, making crazy claims like that?"

Then about half an hour later, they came back on and said, "Two firefighters have fallen through the roof, and crews are searching for them." We all grabbed our gear, jumped in our cars, and raced to the scene to join in the search.

We got there just as they were removing the bodies of Captain David Lau and Trial Firefighter Larry McDonald Jr., both of Engine 26.

The scene was surreal, one that I never will forget. Tearful firefighters were walking around in shock. Every piece of equipment the City could muster was there. Huge lights were set up on both ends of the building. The building was located on the Jeffries Freeway service drive, and the freeway was shut down, and two rescue helicopters had landed there. It always surprises me that in moments like this, our City performs so well.

Engine 26 had responded on third alarm after Paul Schimeck was killed. Captain Lau was a seasoned veteran who had previously been a training instructor at the fire academy. Trial Firefighter McDonald was assigned to Ladder 16. When the run came in for Engine 26, Captain Lau had the young trial man jump on the engine. Most experienced captains would have done the same, this was a big fire, and you want to get the new guys all the fires you can.

The name McDonald is a well-known firefighting name in Detroit. Larry's father is a firefighter; his grandfather was a firefighter. And he has two uncles who also were Detroit firefighters. Larry was a high school basketball star and could have gone to college on a scholarship. Today, he probably would be some successful stockbroker living a comfortable life, but the family calling was too great, and he became a Detroit firefighter.

When Engine 26 arrived, the original vacant structure was fully engulfed in fire. To protect the adjoining occupied building, Continental Paper Company, the chief ordered Engine 26 to the roof with a two-and-a-half-inch line. Captain Lau, TFF McDonald, and a third firefighter were maintaining the line on the roof. Captain Lau told the third firefighter to get them more line. He went back to the roof's edge to pull line, heard a noise, and felt the roof shake. When he looked back, Captain Lau and TFF McDonald were gone. A portion of the fire wall had collapsed, pulling down the section of the roof they were on and then burying them in eight feet of rubble on the bottom floor.

I left Engine10 quarters and headed to Paul's house to see if there was anything I could do. Paul's wife, Karen, and one son were there. What can you say at a time like this? They told me Paul would be laid out at Sajewski Funeral home and asked if I would help out there. "I'd be honored," I said.

Sajewski Funeral home is a well-known funeral home located on Warren Avenue in the old Polish neighborhood. Half of my relatives were laid out there. Polish funerals are very similar to Irish funerals. We both have big, loving wakes.

I stopped by Sajewski's, and they told me that we could do whatever we wanted. In the back, they have a large garage where they keep their hearse and limousine. The garage is cleaner than most living rooms. We moved the vehicles out and set up tables and chairs. Every bar and restaurant in the neighborhood brought food, beverages, and kegs of beer.

All day and night long, the funeral home was packed. Mourners, family, friends, and firefighters from everywhere packed the place. They would go up front and pay their respects then stop out back for some refreshments. The whole time, I'm sure Paul was looking down and having a hearty laugh.

The Detroit Firemen's Fund took care of arranging the massive funeral. It was held downtown. All three firefighters would be laid to rest together. I was walking down the street toward the funeral, turned the corner, and there it was. It hit me like a cold punch—three fire engines parked in a lot. On top, each had a flag-draped coffin. Tears rolled from my eyes as the three rigs started up. Then someone yelled to me, "Jump on!"

The three engines with the flag-draped coffins humbly riding on their hose beds proceeded down Michigan Avenue, bringing Paul, David, and Larry on their last run. The rigs followed one another down

Michigan, and then they made a right on Washington Boulevard and went three abreast.

Turning the corner on Washington Boulevard was a scene that I'll never forget. Thousands of firefighters from everywhere were lined up, wearing their blue dress uniforms with right hands up in a finale salute. We then solemnly proceeded to Cobo Hall.

Inside Cobo, the service was held in the arena. Families were upfront with four thousand firefighters behind them. Behind us in the second tier were our families. The place holds ten thousand, and it was nearly filled.

On the podium, civic leaders from all over Michigan and union leaders from all over America came and offered their condolences. One person noticeably absent was the mayor. Three firefighters killed in the line of duty and Detroit's Mayor Coleman Young didn't attend. I doubt that would happen in any other city.

When the service ended, a couple thousand of us headed north to Casey's Bar and the surrounding bars on Michigan Avenue. Casey's was packed. The union and fund were picking up the tab. Hundreds of firemen from all over America crowded in there, all dressed in dark blue dress uniforms with shoulder patches.

The drinks flowed, and after a while, sadness turned to merriment, as it always happens. I went outside for a breath of fresh air, and I bumped into another fireman.

"How's it going?" I asked.

"Not so good," he responded.

I looked up and saw that it was Larry McDonald, Junior's dad, in his dress uniform with a look on his face that I'll never forget. I told him how sorry I was and then went home.

A few weeks later, a local TV show titled *Second Look* called me up and said they wanted to do a show on the three fallen firefighters. Could I get their families to come? Paul's wife, David Lau's wife, and Larry McDonald's mother all kindly agreed to come.

The show went well with all three telling their thoughts on the difficulties of being the spouse and mother of a firefighter. Afterward, while walking out to the parking lot with the three of them, Larry McDonald's mother turned to me and said, "You know, Bob, he was doing his truck service. If they'd just left him on the truck, my son would still be here."

CHAPTER 21

On December 28, we responded to a dwelling fire with people trapped on Omaha Street in Southwest Detroit. I was on the back end of Ladder 13, strapping on my air tank, getting ready. There is no higher adrenaline rush for firefighters than hearing the words "People trapped." Firefighting is serious business, and when people are trapped, it doesn't get any more serious.

We pulled up to the last house on the street right next to the I-75 freeway. It was a two-story home, and the first floor was on fire. Out front, a lady was shouting that her granddaughter was still upstairs, sleeping.

Engine 33 along with Engine 48 stretched line into the first floor to attack the fire. Another firefighter named Bob Irwin and I grabbed a twenty-foot ladder, threw it up to a second-story window, busted out the window, and crawled in.

The floor was full of heat and smoke. He went right, and I went left. After a long minute or two, Bob yelled, "I found her." I crawled toward his voice, and there she was, an unconscious teenage girl in her nightgown. We picked her up and carried her to the window. We passed her to Mike Simon, who was at the top of the ladder, through the opened window.

The EMS was on the scene and transported her to Detroit Receiving Hospital. We came down the ladder, and the grandmother asked me if her granddaughter was okay. "I think so," I said. It was our standard answer only to give people hope. Word came back later that she died at the hospital.

The two of them were the only ones who lived there. A small, modestly furnished bungalow, that's all they had, that house and each other, and now it was all gone. It's tough to get insurance in that neighborhood, and if you do, it's terribly expensive. Most poor people can't afford it.

Whenever I drive down I-75 into the city, I pass by that neighborhood, and I remember that cold December night. I wonder how the grandmother is doing and how she coped with her sad loss. It always seemed to me that poorer people accepted life and its tragedies better than the rest of us.

I think of my own children and how lucky they are. They grew up in a safe neighborhood where fires never happen, in a house where their parents had decent jobs and could provide for them. Not like that poor granddaughter. If only we could have gotten there a little sooner.

They gave us both a citation for that rescue, my second one, another ribbon for my dress uniform. How important all that stuff seemed to me at the time. Looking back, I can't help but to feel a bit uncomfortable.

The year 1988 was an election year, and for the first time, I got involved in a presidential election, for the primary anyway. Dick Gephardt, a senator from Missouri, was running on a protectionist platform. He had a TV commercial showing that a Chrysler K car that costs $12,000 in the United States costs $48,000 in Japan. Finally, I thought, someone concerned about the US auto industry.

I spent a few days at his Michigan campaign headquarters, stuffing envelopes, making phone calls, and doing other general stuff. I even met some of his family.

I was back at the union office for our monthly board meeting when a call for me came in. It was the Gephardt campaign office inviting me to dinner with Dick Gephardt at Carl's Chop House. I figured this must be some kind of big pep rally and told them I would be there.

Always after a board meeting, we go out for dinner. This night we went to Sinbad's, a seafood restaurant on the river. I had my usual perch dinner, and then I headed for home. As I was driving, I remembered Gephardt at Carl's. I turned my car around and headed for Carl's.

When I pulled up to Carl's, I gulped. Parked out front were a half a dozen black Chevy Suburbans with a bunch of big guys in suits talking into their wristwatches. Dick Gephardt had just won the Iowa primary, making him, at the time, one of the most powerful men in America. I parked my car and ran in. "Where's Gephardt?" I shouted to the hostess. She pointed, and I ran in that direction toward a couple of closed doors.

I opened the door and jumped in, and as soon as I did, I tried to jump back out. Inside was not at all as I expected. Instead of some big rally, the whole room was cleared out. In the center of this large room was one table with ten chairs, nine people sitting, and one chair empty.

As I tried to get out, a large man in a suit grabbed me and said, "What the heck do you think you're doing?"

Then another person from the table came running over and said, "Hey, it's Bob Dombrowski. Come on in."

I clearly wasn't ready for this. I was dressed in jeans and a DFD union jacket. He took me to the table and introduced me then sat me in the empty seat right across Dick Gephardt. They were all wearing suits, and they were just ordering their food. I ordered the same thing Mr. Gephardt ordered, which was pork chops and a cold Bud. I had already eaten, but I was too embarrassed to admit this.

Sitting at the end of the table was a United Automobile Workers vice president. They did not endorse Gephardt. Instead, they endorsed his rival, Michael Dukakis. I looked at him and said, "Dick Gephardt has made the American autoworkers a central part of his campaign and you guys endorse Dukakis? Do you think there will ever be another presidential candidate going out on the limb for the American autoworkers after this?"

When I got home from the Gephardt dinner, I ran upstairs, woke up my wife, and said, "You'll never guess who I had dinner with tonight!"

"Probably Dick Gephardt," she said.

"How did you know?"

"Oh just a wild guess. Now let me go back to sleep."

"I brought you a pork chop," I said.

The next morning at work, I got a call from our union leader. "What the heck did you say to the UAW last night?" I told him, and he wasn't pleased. In the end, Dukakis won the primary then lost to Bush. I still think Gephardt had a better chance of winning. Buy American!

CHAPTER 22

1988

The year 1988 was the year I built a home outside the city and then moved my family into it. We had bought a lot on an island twenty miles south of Detroit a few years earlier. We initially bought it for an investment, but our financial conditions improved, and we decided to build.

By moving out of the City, I could be in violation of the city's residency rule and could be fired. We would joke about how it seemed that there was nothing you could get fired for in Detroit except living outside the City. Not only was I a firefighter who was breaking the residency rule, I was also a union director and one of the main persons responsible for the residency bill in Lansing. My friends thought I was nuts for moving out and I would probably get fired!

But first things first, I had to sell my house in Detroit. I lived in a neighborhood called Copper Canyon with all City employees. Putting that For Sale sign up was one of the hardest things I ever did. Fortunately, I didn't have to keep the sign up long. One hour after putting up the For Sale sign, a young lady knocked on the door and bought the house. That was the great thing about Copper Canyon; folks were always looking for houses there.

Next, I had to get myself a place to live in Detroit to keep my residence or to play the game, as we called it. A firefighter was selling his mother's house in Southwest Detroit on Lawndale Street for a very good price. I bought it and had a Detroit cop move in with me.

Playing the game was not that easy. We put everything on Grosse Ile, our suburban house, in my wife's name. The house, taxes, insurance, and utilities were all in Linda's name. Everything that was in my name, including my auto insurance and my voting card, was listed at my Detroit address.

My uniforms never left Detroit. I would leave work at the fire station and drive to my Detroit home to take a shower and change clothes before heading to Grosse Ile. When coming to work, I would leave the Grosse Ile home by 11:00 p.m. and head to Lawndale Street, where I would spend the night before going to work. I did this every single workday.

As hard as that might seem, it was harder for Bill, my Detroit cop roommate. Firefighters only work eight days a month, eight twenty-four-hour days, but still only eight. Cops, on the other hand, work five days a week. So Bill would have to stay in the city all week and only go home on weekends to see his family.

The home on Lawndale Street was in a tough neighborhood. The reason my firefighter friend sold it to me was because of all the break-ins. Going there every night at eleven was no picnic. I would try to find a parking spot close-by then jog to the house. Once inside, I felt okay. I had bars on the windows and a 12-gauge shotgun under my bed.

Then I had to worry about someone turning me in for residency. We would say that the average person didn't know what day of the week it was or who the president of the United States was, but they knew that if you were a cop or a fireman, you had to live in the City.

I called it question A and question B. Whenever folks found out that I owned a home in the suburbs, they would usually start with question A, "Aren't you a Detroit firefighter?" And then question B followed, "Aren't you supposed to live in Detroit?" Then I would explain to them that I do live in the City. These were just mild, little threats that I would have to live with.

But what choice did I have? I had a wife and three kids. Crime was getting worse, the schools were terrible, and your best investment in life is usually your home. I worked hard and should be able to enjoy the benefits of my labor like all other Americans. And my wife had her own job and worked hard too. She should be able to live where she chooses.

By playing the game, you weren't really living like an American. You had to watch what you said and look over your shoulder as you left the city because they would follow you. You told your kids "Don't tell anyone that Daddy is a fireman." Good luck keeping that secret.

But nobody enjoys spending a little time in a quiet, peaceful suburb more than a Detroit firefighter. After a tough night in the city, I would drive across that bridge, and suddenly, I would be at peace. It would be this ying and yang of life that would keep me going.

Another Detroit firefighter who had a home close-by was a person that I'll call Lieutenant Hank. Hank not only had a suburban home close to mine but, for a while, ran at the same fire station, Engine 33.

When Hank first showed up at Engine 33, he had a strange way of introducing himself. He sat down at the table across from me and asked me if I was all right.

"Sure, I'm all right," I said.

"How do you know? Do you have a paper saying you're all right?" Hank asked.

He then reached into his uniform shirt pocket and pulled out a folded, yellowed piece of paper. He unfolded it and showed me this form signed by a psychiatrist saying that he was sane and fit for duty.

"You got one of these?" he asked. "If you don't, then how do you know that you're all right?"

Turns out, Hank was removed from the job over an altercation he had a few years back at an east-side fire station. The story is that he tried attacking a chief that he had a disagreement with. The cops were called, and it took half a dozen of them to cuff him and haul him away. Hank was not one to mess with. He was well over six feet tall and as strong as a bear. He was a bricklayer on his days off.

Hank was fired over that incident. It took him a long time to get back on. He got back on the job after a psychiatrist wrote a letter saying that he wasn't crazy. That's the paper that he carried in his shirt pocket.

Hank was one of the most talented guys I ever met. From building telescopes to owning race horses, Hank did it all. Days were never boring with Hank on duty. Water fights, plate fights, cup fights, fistfights, something happened every day with Lieutenant Hank.

We had a fire on the fifth floor of a senior citizen high-rise. On high-rise fires, we take the stairs up to the floor below the fire floor, hook the hose line up to the standpipe, turn the standpipe on, then proceed up to fight the fire. When no water comes out, as was the case this time, we then radio down for the engine hooked up to the standpipe to supply us water.

Standpipes are those brass fittings you see sticking out of buildings with signs saying For Fire Department Use. They are fittings for water pipes that run all along the building. The fire engine hooks up a hose to a fire hydrant then a hose to the standpipe and starts filling it up with water. That's how they get firemen the water to extinguish the fire in high-rises and big buildings that don't have working fire pumps.

While waiting for water, we crawled down the hallway through the smoke, dragging the limp line. We reached the burning apartment and patiently waited in the smoky hallway for our water. They must be having problems outside, we thought, because it was taking so long.

Then we heard the sound of breaking glass and water hitting the fire. "Someone's in there," I said. We slowly opened the apartment door, only to be greeted by a water spray right in the face mask. We got up, walked in, and found two firefighters putting out the fire. I looked out the window and saw a fifty-foot ladder practically flat against the wall.

They had crawled up the fifty-foot ladder five stories, carrying an axe in one hand and pulling the red line in another, busted out the window, and climbed in.

"Are you guys nuts?" I asked.

"We're not, but maybe someone else is," they said. Climbing in behind them was Lieutenant Hank.

A couple days later, I came in to work and looked for a cup of coffee, but there wasn't any.

"Where are all the coffee cups?" I asked.

One of the guys just pointed to Lieutenant Hank, who was sitting by himself at the table. It turns out, the day before, Hank used the cups like Skee-Balls at a carnival, throwing them at the guys, while they dodged for their life.

I sat down at the table across from the lieutenant and asked him in a nice way, "You going to replace the cups?" Most of the guys wouldn't do this because they were afraid of Hank, but I knew Hank wouldn't punch me.

"Maybe it's time that you transferred out of here," he said.

Hank did replace all the cups, which he broke again a couple of months later. And I did transfer out because I was about to make sergeant.

Ed Powers and me in our clown outfits at old Tiger's Stadium for the Fireman's Field Day.

My last day as a Battalion Chief.

Receiving a citation at Fire Headquarters.

Governor Engler signing the residency bill.

Walking into the World Trade Center site.

The Detroit Fire Department clown team coming down Woodward for the Thanksgiving Parade.

The double bottom tanker crash where I earned my first citation.

Me as a sergeant working an apartment fire.

A group of Detroit Firefighters at a FDNY fire fighters' funeral in Long Island.

Engine 10 and Ladder 4 showing off there brand new rigs.

A bunch of us off-duty at Casey's Bar having fun with shaving cream.

Sadly escorting Lt. Shimeck on his last ride.

A young Ron Winchester and me at Ladder 13. We were reunited again at the end of my career when we were the two Senior Chiefs of the DFD.

Getting ready to holler "chow" at Engine 33 quarters.

One of Detroit's legendary Seagrave "Safety Cabs". This style Rig was designed by the Detroit Fire Department and was used exclusively by us for over 30 years.

12th Street during the 1967 Riots.

Detroit Fire Department's Headquarters.

The boat tender. Its top mounted water cannons are over 100 years old.

A 1970's style squad rig. Detroit was the first city in America to employ squad companies. They were originally called "Flying Squads".

Ventilating a roof at a dwelling fire.

Two firefighters going up an ariel.

Using roof ladders and the ariel to open up a roof.

Firefighters on the stick.

Old Seagrave at a Blvd. Fire.

Devil's Night fire.

Two dwellings on fire on Devil's night with no available fire trucks for 30 minutes.

Early morning dwelling fire
in the 7th Battalion.

Firefighter rescuing a child from a burning apartment.

Detroit's famous Buhl Building fire where they spliced ladders to perform necessary rescues.

CHAPTER 23

1989

On June 6, 1989, I was promoted to sergeant, a couple weeks shy of my seventeenth anniversary. This was halftime in my career. I spent seventeen years as a firefighter; the next twenty-one years would be spent as an officer.

What a great day this was. The chief took me downtown, and the commissioner presented me with my sergeant badge. I was thirty-eight years old and couldn't be happier.

Sergeant, they say, is just a fill-in officer, a substitute teacher, some call it, but after seventeen years of riding the back end, it would be my favorite promotion. I would now ride in the front seat of the rig. No longer would I have to do dishes or stand watches. I would wear a light blue shirt with a badge on it. My helmet would be painted red. And I got a 10 percent pay raise.

I was transferred to Ladder 4. It was in the same battalion, the Seventh. They had to keep me there because I was still the Seventh Battalion union director.

I lucked out because the captain was acting chief every day, so I would stay there and be in charge. Back then, we ran with only three on the truck. The crew consisted of an officer; me, a detailed driver; the regular driver, detailed to drive an engine every day; and China. China was a female firefighter about five feet three inches tall and weighed a little over a hundred pounds soaking wet. She was a trial firefighter detailed to Ladder 4 for the next two months for her truck service.

It was probably not an all-star crew to be handed to a new sergeant who hoped to do well, but it was what I had, and I would make it work. China was small in size, but she made up for it in energy. As far as my driver, it was a new one every day.

Few jobs are harder at working fires than the jobs that truck crews have. Most of Detroit's fires are dwelling fires. You got three engines that did engine work, one squad who also usually did engine work, and one truck crew that did all the truck work. The truck is responsible for opening the doors then busting out the windows then putting up the ladders and opening up the roof. Trucks also do rescue with just three firefighters.

After all the doors, windows, and roofs were opened, we would put our axes down, grab pike poles, go inside, and start opening walls and ceilings. That is after we shut off all the utilities coming into the house. This was very important because you didn't want anyone to get electrocuted.

When the fire was finally knocked down, the truck crew got salvage covers off their rig and covered up the furniture, if there was any furniture. Then at the very end, right after we put all our tools and ladders away, I would get a pen and a piece of paper to write down all the information. Information consisted of finding who the homeowner was, did they have insurance, and how did the fire start. Truck crews also were the ones who were responsible for all the fire reports.

Now China didn't know any of this stuff. She was just a trial firefighter who had spent her first three months on an engine. So it was also my job to teach her. Teaching and doing at the same time can be very frustrating, especially when you're dealing with burning buildings. But what really made my job hard as the new Ladder 4 sergeant was dealing with my chief, Wild Joe Kellog.

Chief Kellog was a bigger-than-life firefighter whose wild reputation preceded him. He came from an old Irish family of firefighters,

In his younger days, he would walk into bars on Vernor Highway and take on the whole bar. Many times they sent the squad to pull him out.

But now, Joe Kellog was a battalion chief, my battalion chief, and he seemed to have it in for me. At every fire he screamed my name. "Sergeant Dombrowski, why isn't the roof opened? Why isn't the power pulled? Where are the salvage covers?" On and on the yelling continued. I would stop engine crews as they ran toward the fire and say, "I need help!" They would see Chief Kellog and know what I was going through and would always help me out.

But Chief Kellog was a hell of a firefighter who loved the truck work best. And he demanded his truck crews only do truck work. This was important because we usually got just one truck at a working fire, and if the truck guys jumped on a hose line, which often happened, then you had nobody doing the truck work.

I would have school every day with China. I would find a vacant dwelling, and we would throw up ground ladders and then carry up roof ladders, and I showed her how we chopped holes in roofs.

One hot July afternoon, we had two two-story dwellings going on Junction just south of Buchanon. We threw up a thirty-footer and a roof ladder, climbed up, and opened up the roof. After a couple large holes in the roof, we were exhausted. We put our tools down and rested for a couple of minutes on the roof peak.

The dwelling next door was also on fire; we were the only truck on the scene. Chief Kellog expected us to climb down from our dwelling, put the ladders up on the next dwelling, climb up, and open up that roof too.

"Fuck that," said my crew. They were exhausted.

I could hear Chief Kellog screaming. "Sergeant Dombrowski, what are you doing up there?" I took my crew to the rear of the roof so we were out of sight. Chief Kellog kept shouting, "Sergeant Dombrowski." Next thing I knew, Chief Kellog was up the ladder then on the roof. He found us and asked, "What the hell are you guys doing?"

"Sorry, Chief, my crew needs a break," I said.

Chief Kellog looked at my exhausted crew and, to my surprise, said, "All right, Sergeant." He climbed back down and found some other unlucky crew to open up that second dwelling's roof.

We had a vacant five-story apartment on fire; all five floors were on fire. This would normally be a three-alarm fire, but not today. Kellog kept it to one alarm. There were five floors with five fire companies, one company per floor; mine was the third floor. We were there for four hours of extreme work. When we picked up, the only part of me that wasn't soot black were my eyeballs.

We had a huge pile of something burning right on the vacant riverbank. Nothing was around, and the fire wasn't going anywhere, plus the closest hydrant was a quarter mile away. Most chiefs would have just let it burn, but not Kellog. We stretched three engines of every foot of line that they had. Afterward, we had to drag over two thousand feet of line a quarter mile through the snow and mud. We called it Kellog's Death March. We looked like the Germans retreating from the Russian front. We felt like them too.

Through it all, I learned to be a truck boss, even if the training was a little too rough. One night, Ladder 4 responded to a vacant, two-story dwelling fire. When we got on the scene, the dwelling was completely engulfed in flames coming through the roof. There was a vacant lot on both sides and a vacant lot behind it. My crew and I were standing in front of the burning dwelling when Chief Kellog pulled up.

"What are you doing, Sergeant Dombrowski?" Kellog asked.

"Nothing, Chief, I'm just standing here, watching the fire," I answered.

"Well, what should you be doing?"

"Nothing, Chief, there's nothing for the truck to do at the moment," I said.

"You're learning, Sergeant Dombrowski, you're learning," said a laughing Chief Kellog.

CHAPTER 24

The fire station I was running at in 1989 was Engine 33. Engine 33 was located on Lawndale Street between Olivet and Lafayette. Right around the corner from Engine33's quarters down on Olivet Street, there were a bunch of vacant lots, not surprisingly.

These lots weren't always vacant, and like so many burnt-out blocks in the city of Detroit, they all had a story to tell. The vacant lot on the corner of Olivet and Elsmere was a corner store that had burned down. The next two houses had each burned down. On this particular night, we were fighting a fire at the third house.

The house was burning pretty good when we pulled up. We were doing our usual, attacking the fire, saving what we could, and all the while protecting the exposures, which was the fourth house. After the fire was out and we were picking up the line, a member of my crew called me over to the fourth house.

Once inside, I was very impressed at how nice it was. The woodwork was beautiful, and it was very tastefully decorated. I was introduced to the homeowner and his lovely wife. They had three children. Then he told me his terrible story.

They were living in terror. The punk kids standing on the sidewalk across the street had just threatened him. They said that they had lit the house next door on fire and the next house they would burn would be his.

I walked across the street to talk to the young punks. I went up to one who looked like the leader and said, "The people across the street said you told them that you're the one who lit that house and you're going to burn their house next."

"They told you that?" he said. "Well, go tell them that not only am I going to burn their house down but I'm going to do it with all of them inside. I hope I kill them all!"

I had seen a lot in my career, but I had never confronted someone so audacious. I knew this was Detroit, where law and order mean little, but this was beyond my understanding.

I promised him in tough words that if anything happened to that family or their home, I would see that he paid for it. I then called for the arson squad, but as usual, none were available.

When I returned to quarters, I called and finally talked to the arson squad and told them what had happened. The next day, I called the chief of Arson, and he assured me action would be taken.

About a week later, I was at a working fire on Thaddeus Street in Southwest Detroit. The fire was knocked down, and we were picking up, and Arson happened to be on the scene. They asked me about the incident the week before on Olivet Street. Just then, a box alarm came over the radio: "Olivet and Elsmere."

"Is that the place?" they asked.

"Yes," I shouted and jumped on the rig.

When we pulled up, I couldn't believe what I saw. The fourth house was in flames, and standing right across the street was the same group of punk kids with the one who made the threats standing defiantly right in the center.

I jumped out of the truck and ran right for him, grabbing him by his collar. I wanted to kill him. I screamed, "You did it. You lit that house on fire just like you said you would. You're one bad motherfucker." I wanted to punch him just then when two firemen grabbed my arms.

The arson crew pulled up and ran over between us and asked, "Is this the guy?"

"Yep, that's him. He told me that he was going to burn that house. He burned it, and he's standing right in front of it!" I said.

"I didn't light that house," the punk said.

"You're a damn liar," I screamed.

The arson squad told me that they would take care of it, so I walked away and went to work on the fire. Luckily, the family made it out safely, but their house and most of their possessions were destroyed.

After the fire was knocked down and we were picking up line, I saw the arson squad guys standing there without the punk kid. "Where is he?" I asked. "Is he dead? Did you guys shoot him and throw his body in the river? Or is he locked up in some dungeon?"

"No, Bob, we had to let him go," they said.

"What? You let that piece of shit go!" I said.

Then they explained to me that the guy had a whole bunch of witnesses who would swear that they were with him and that he didn't do it. There wasn't anything they could do about it.

"Besides," they asked, "would he be dumb enough to tell you he was going to burn down that house then let you find him standing in front of it if he did light it?"

"Yes, he is that dumb and that evil," I said.

Well, that was it. What little faith I had in humanity was now gone. That little punk told me he was going to burn that family's house. He did it, and now he was getting away with it. I was devastated, and the arson squad knew it. I knew they had it rough, so I couldn't really blame them. With all the fires and being understaffed, they had to go after the cases they had the best chances of winning.

The captain of the arson squad heard about the incident on Olivet, and my anger and got involved. On his own time after work, he would park his car in the alley on Olivet Street. He did this night after night for weeks. Then one night he got lucky. He saw our friend with a can of gas trying to light another house. He jumped out of his car, arrested him, and the judge threw the book at him. Thanks to that captain, my faith in humanity was somewhat restored.

The City tried to send our squads on medical runs. The squads were already too busy with all the fire runs, but people were waiting too long for an EMS, and they wanted the squads to help out. The union was against this. The EMS handled all the medical runs. Firemen did not do medical runs in Detroit. We were too busy fighting fires. So when the city tried to send the squads on medical runs, the union took action.

Detroit's EMS is the busiest EMS in the country. Depending on the day, the City had twenty-five to thirty EMS rigs on duty covering the city. Many EMS rigs average twenty-four runs a day. That's twenty-four runs in a twenty-four-hour period. The EMS is so busy that the wait for an EMS can be an hour long. The media was constantly doing horror stories about people dying while waiting for an EMS.

Detroit's answer to the long-wait problem was to send our six squads on medical runs. The media jumped on the bandwagon. Why shouldn't the squads help the EMS? People were dying, and they were just sitting around the engine house. Never mind that the squads averaged two or three working fires a day plus handled all the car wrecks and a lot of other stuff.

The media and the city, as always, made it look like the union was the bad guy. "Because of some stupid contract language, the union wasn't letting the squads make any medical runs," they said. It was an unpopular fight with the general public, but we needed our squads for fighting fires. In the end, the union won. Firefighters would not have to make medical runs, at least for now. The union won, but it gave the public another reason to bad-mouth unions.

CHAPTER 25

1990s

During the 1980s and the 1990s, Engine 33 and Ladder 13 on Lawndale Street in the Seventh Battalion was one of the busiest areas in Detroit for fires. I'm sure that it's still very busy, but now, the entire City is busy.

This would be a typical summer day at Engine 33. I would get to work around 7:00 a.m. The apparatus doors would be wide open. I would walk in, and the first thing I would notice was the smell of smoke. I knew right away that, as usual, they were up all night, fighting fires. Placed all along the return wall would be broken equipment, axes, pike poles, lengths of line, air harnesses, and other equipment that was broke at the last night's fires, waiting to be taken to the shop and replaced.

I'd then proceed into the kitchen, which would be littered with plates, pots, pans, and half-eaten food. Then I would walk into the dining area. Sitting around the table, sipping coffee, and smoking cigarettes would be the other unit, waiting to go home. They would be filthy dirty with wet T-shirts and bloodshot eyes.

"Busy night?" I would jokingly ask.

"Man, we got our asses kicked last night!" That would be their usual response.

They had been up all night, fighting fires, and that's all they would say. "We got our asses kicked." If you pressed the issue, you might get "Well, we had a dwelling on Mason Place, a commercial building in Delray, and they lit that apartment on Vernor Highway again."

Despite all the fires Detroit gets, the guys don't talk about them that much. I was always amazed at how well a suburban firefighter could describe his last fire in detail. Sometimes they could talk for an hour about a particular fire, describing every phase. In Detroit, that same fire would be defined as "We had a dwelling on Mason Place," nothing more.

Slowly, one by one the boys would get up and head for home, where they would try to get some sleep before tomorrow's shift, leaving us with their mess. "We need everything" would be their parting words. This meant that we needed fuel for the rig, air for our air tanks, plus switching all the broken tools.

After they left, we cleaned the entire fire station. Then we cleaned and checked the fire trucks. Then we did the paperwork, and after that, we headed out. Our first stop would be Engine27's quarters to fill up our air tanks and drop off the paperwork. We then went to the DPW yard and filled up with diesel fuel. After that, we headed down to the repair shop to replace our broken equipment. Hopefully, they had replacement equipment available.

Then we checked and pumped hydrants or chopped weeds or did some other job that the city had come up with for us. Around noon, we headed back to quarters for an enormous lunch. We then went upstairs for what we hoped would be a couple of hours of uninterrupted sleep.

A couple of hours later, we woke up, came downstairs, grabbed a cup of coffee, and waited for the madness to start. In the summer, it usually started with us having to go out and shut off hydrants that people illegally turned on. That was always fun. People called us names, threw things at us, and sometimes even attacked us. "People are just trying to cool off, but the firemen won't let them," they would yell at us.

A lucky summer day was when we didn't have a daytime fire because few things are worse than fighting fires in the hot sun. The temperature in burning buildings can reach up to two thousand degrees.

The fire gear we wear is as warm as a snowsuit. We would come out of the building after fighting the fire with steam puffing off us. We would fall down on the ground, strip off our fire gear, and other firemen would then turn the hoses on and drench us off with cool water. We would just lay there in total exhaustion.

As the evening rolled in, so did the box alarms, and off you went, run after run, fire after fire, all night long. Before you knew it, it was daylight and you're sitting at the table, filthy dirty and soaking wet, sipping a cup of coffee, when the other unit walked in.

"Busy night?" they'd jokingly ask.

"Man, we got our asses kicked!" we'd say.

One busy hot summer night, we finally made it to bed at around 5:00 a.m. when the alert went off. "Box alarm, Lucas Restaurant on Oakwood!" the man on watch shouted out. Lucas Restaurant, I hope they're wrong, I thought. Lucas was the nicest place in Southwest Detroit, an old Italian restaurant Frank Sinatra used to frequent whenever he was in town. *It must be a false alarm. We'll be back in ten minutes.*

But my hope was not to be. When we pulled up, smoke was oozing out the front door. I ordered the guys to stretch and sent the engine to the hydrant. We kicked in the front door and crawled in through the heavy smoke with an uncharged line. It is very dangerous to enter a building before the lines are charged with water, but it's easier to pull an uncharged line through. Also, we wanted to attack this fire as soon as we could to try to save this place.

Now, as most firefighters will agree, the most dangerous part of fighting a fire is when you can't see the fire and don't know where it is. If that fire got between you and your exit, you could be in big trouble. We crawled around the restaurant, knocking over tables and chairs, looking for the fire.

Toward the back of the restaurant, we opened the ceiling, and there was the fire right over our heads. All we needed now was water. Where was it? Just then, my engineer (driver) radioed us and said she had a bad hydrant and we'd better get out.

"That's just perfect," I said.

We knew we shouldn't have been in there without a charged line, but this was a nice restaurant, and we took a chance. *If we leave now*, I thought, *by the time we get water and get back to this spot, the fire will be coming through the roof.* We all agreed to stay and wait for water. After a long and hot minute or two, the water came, and we saved most of the restaurant.

When we came out after putting out the fire, the owner, Mama Luca, was there. Somebody told her what we did. "Thank you," she said. "We are going to rebuild this restaurant, and on the day we open, I'm going to have all you firefighters as my guests."

Wow, I thought, she was going to bring us all to dinner when she reopens! Things like that rarely happen to Detroit firefighters. They happen in most other cities, but not Detroit. Nobody ever took us out after saving their business. In other cities, firemen get free movie tickets, free hockey tickets, free football tickets, even free meals at restaurants, but not us. In fact, of the thousands of fires I've been to, I can count on one hand the times someone handed me a can of pop. But this time, we were all going to dinner.

Of course, it never happened. She must have forgotten, but it was nice that she thanked us. The Lucas family did rebuild their restaurant right on that same spot. As a Detroiter, I'm happy about that.

CHAPTER 26

It was a nice Saturday morning in May, one of those beautiful spring days that makes you happy to be in Michigan. The Saturday-morning apparatus-room flush-out was completed, and we had just sat down for a cup of coffee and a donut, which the cook had just arrived with, when the phone rang.

It was the chief, and he told me that we had to go and help some suburban school kids who came down to the City to convert a vacant lot into a park. "Oh shit" was the reaction of the crew when I told them the good news.

"The chief says all that we have to do is water," I said.

"Sure, we know how that goes."

We piled onto the rig and headed to the location. This happens a lot in the City. Do-gooders give up their weekend and come to the hood to make a difference, as they say. And we seemed to always end up having to join in. There goes our downtime, I thought.

When we pulled up, I recognized the location immediately. A year or two earlier, we had stretched on two dwellings going throughout right there. The two vacant lots were now cleared of the burned buildings, and parked in front was a school bus with Birmingham Schools written on the side. Standing on the lots were a couple dozen clean-cut suburban kids ready to go to work with rakes and shovels. With them were a couple of eager-beaver teachers giving us welcoming smiles as we pulled up.

Just off the street, there were a bunch of little trees, several landscape timbers, a park bench, and a pile of dirt that some landscape company must have dropped off. Before you knew it, everyone was working away at planting trees, picking up trash, raking leaves, trying to turn those vacant lots into a nice little pocket park.

The firemen, despite all their complaints, jumped right in. Many of the kids had never worked on landscaping like this before, and the firemen were happy to teach them. Firemen are always like this. They might complain like hell, but when it comes time for them to work, they are more than pleased to help out.

As we were working, I noticed a few of the local boys milling around on the corner while keeping a curious eye on us. In this neighborhood, most of the young folk belong in one of two gangs, the Latin Counts or the Cobras. These kids were wearing blue, so I think that they were Counts. After about a half hour, a group of four walked over.

"What's going on?" one of them asked.

"What's going on?" A smiling teacher ran over, extending his hand for a welcoming shake. "Well, we're all here on this beautiful Saturday afternoon from Birmingham, working to turn this vacant lot into a nice park for you guys. Here, I'll introduce you to everybody." And with that, he called all the students over and began introducing them.

Now, the firemen, out of amused curiosity, dropped their shovels and strolled over to watch. The teacher went on introducing his students, hoping, I thought, for some kind of a meaningful encounter. Then the teacher asked them if they would like to join and help with their park.

"What are you going to pay us?" one of them asked.

"Pay? Oh no," said the smiling teacher. "no, we're all volunteers. Nobody is getting paid. We do this for free!"

"We do this for free!" the one youth responded, and they all looked at each other and laughed. As they walked away, I could hear them mocking the teacher's words, "We do this for free!"

Well, that went well, I thought, and the students went back to work, all the wiser, unfortunately.

On October 28, 1990, two days before Devil's Night, I earned a citation for a rescue in Southwest Detroit on South Street. I was in charge of Engine 33. We responded to a box alarm on South. When we pulled up, Engine 29 was stretched on a burning two-flat. I looked up at the house, and I could see that the upstairs was heavily engulfed in fire.

I was jogging up while snapping on my MSA harness and saw a man shouting that his child was still in the house. I grabbed his arm, and I asked him to point to his child's bedroom window. He pointed to a window on the right side of the second story.

Engine 29 had stretched a one-and-a-half-inch line up the back stairway; I followed it up to the top of the stairs where the crew was battling the fire. I put my mask on and crawled past them to my left. I stayed close to the wall, and with water spraying me, I crawled through the smoke, feeling for a bedroom door.

It's not that easy finding something when the smoke is so thick you can't see, plus you're scared of getting trapped in the fire. I found a door, pushed it open, crawled in, and I felt the crib. I reached in, and there he was, a little two-year-old child. Yes, I got him!

I picked him up, holding him in front of me and keeping my back toward the fire. I dove toward the streaming water. I yelled to the guys, "Let me through," and I ran with the little guy down the steps. The EMS was just pulling up, so I ran toward them. One of the techs jumped out of the rig and took him from me. He was covered with smoke, and he wasn't breathing. The EMS got him breathing again and began preparing to transport him to the hospital.

I stood there, watching them as they backed down the street, turned, and sped off to the hospital. It is hard to tell you how good you feel after performing a rescue like that. It doesn't happen every day. It is something every fireman thinks about every day but many never get to experience.

I looked up at the dwelling. Water was spraying out the front window. The fire was knocked down. They were starting to overhaul, using axes and pike poles to pull the ceilings and walls apart to look for more fire. I got a pole off the rig and went back up the stairs.

CHAPTER 27

A fun part of being a union director is that every two years the International Association of Fire Fighters has a convention, and if you're lucky, you get to attend. I loved the conventions. They were always first class. I met firemen from all over America. My favorites were the firemen from Northern California. They seemed to live the good life.

Not only were the conventions a great learning experience but they were a good time. Every night the IAFF had a different event planned for our entertainment. After that, there were the hospitality rooms that were usually packed with firefighters drinking and socializing until the wee hours.

The 1990 IAFF Convention was held in Saint Louis. The IAFF had a request for Detroit. They wanted us to bid for the 1994 convention. The 1992 Convention was scheduled for Vancouver, Canada. The reason the IAFF wanted Detroit to try to get the convention was that Detroit was one of the only cities left that still had union hotel workers.

Sure, we thought. We were Detroit, and we could do anything. We formed a three-man committee to try and get the convention.

The three of us went over to the Detroit Convention Bureau in the Renaissance Center, a sharp-looking office filled with cool people. They got very excited when we told them what we planned to do.

That's what these people at the convention bureau do. They work hard to bring conventions to the city of Detroit, not the easiest job in the world. But they couldn't be more helpful. They pointed out all the wonderful attractions we have around Detroit and all the resources that would help us. "How cool it would be to have the Firefighters Convention in Detroit," they said.

Next, we met with a person that I'll call Joe, who was from New York. He had a company that set up conventions for different unions including the IAFF. He immediately brought us down to earth. He told us that there were three other cities bidding for the 1994 Convention: Seattle, Las Vegas, and San Francisco. We were in fourth place. The reason we were in fourth was that there were four cities. If a fifth city should decide to bid, then Detroit would drop to fifth. Nobody wanted to come to Detroit. He was honest; we were known as the murder capital of the Rust Belt, and a bunch of other mean and nasty things.

This convention became a challenge for us, and nobody accepts a challenge better than a Detroit firefighter. Sure, we understood why they would rather go to those other cities. But we are a city too, and we have union hotel workers here, and they didn't. Somehow we were going to win.

It is remarkable to see what Detroiters do when faced with a challenge, how hard we work and how clever we can be. You would never know it driving around some of these old dumpy streets but there is a lot of talent here.

When we got to Saint Louis, those other cities, as popular as they were, didn't have a chance against us Detroiters. Stroh's Beer, which was still located in Downtown Detroit, gave us seven hundred cases of beer. Little Caesars Pizza, who's headquarters is also located in Downtown Detroit, sent us a big semi-truck that turned into a mobile pizza oven that served two thousand pizzas an hour, all for free!

We fed them lunch at noon and got them loaded at night. They loved us. The Detroit Convention Bureau showed up in force and brought beautiful displays from all our local attractions. It was nothing short of astonishing. Our competition showed up with little more than a smile and a brochure or two. Nobody expected Detroit to pull off what we did.

When the vote came down, it was a mandate they were coming to Detroit! So what if we didn't have all the glitter that the other three cities had. We were union, and it was time that they came to a union city. Afterward, a few of the boys were a little uneasy. How would they tell their wives that they voted to go to Detroit instead of San Francisco or Vegas?

"Don't worry, brother," I told them, "you did the right thing."

Shortly after we returned home as the conquering heroes, the firemen that won the convention, we found out that Hollywood was making a movie about firefighters called *Backdraft*.

Around every fifteen years, it seems, you can look forward to Hollywood making a new movie about firefighters. First there was the *Towering Inferno* in 1974. Then came *Backdraft* in 1991. The next movie was *Ladder 49* in 2004, and around the year 2019, there should be a new firefighters movie, maybe about Detroit.

This was 1991, and *Backdraft* was coming out soon, and we figured that a bunch of PR experts, like us who won the IAFF Convention, could get in on the action. We could have a big fund-raiser, have a premier showing, and give the movie a lot of good publicity.

We contacted the Fox Theater, an old beautiful theater in Downtown Detroit, to see if they wanted to get involved, and they were all for it. We contacted everyone else: vendors, media, and the department, and everyone thought that it was a great idea. Lastly, we contacted the movie people in Hollywood.

We told them what we wanted to do, and they said that they weren't interested. I was surprised; we could have given them all the PR, especially having it on a Thursday, the day before its usual Friday opening.

"We would have every local news station there covering the event. The whole street would be lined with fire trucks. Firemen from all over the metro area would be there. Plus we would help raise money for charity!" I told her.

"Every fireman will see the movie anyway," she said.

"Yes, but if only firemen see the movie, it will be a flop. This will be free advertisement to the general public, and all the work will be done by us at no cost to you," I told her.

But it was all a waste of time. The movie people had no interest in our event. How miserable, I thought, that those people in Hollywood who represent the film industry, one of the most creative industries in America, had so little imagination and initiative. Hollywood people are lucky they don't have to compete with Detroit people. Just look at the convention.

One of the jobs a union director had to do was to make monthly rounds. Once a month, right after the monthly board meeting, you'd visit all your stations twice, once on each unit, and hold an informal engine house meeting to bring them up to date on all the recent union activities.

In the Seventh Battalion, there were five stations plus the fireboat, which meant I had twelve stops. I would spend an hour or two at each fire station, bringing them up to date and listening to their problems or ideas.

I was doing my rounds. I was at Engine 48, and I was about halfway through with my presentation when a firefighter I'll call James stood up and pointed his finger at me and said, "You live on Grosse Ile!" Everybody was shocked at James's brazen statement. He had accused me in public of being in violation of Detroit's residency law. The penalty is firing.

"No, you're wrong. I live in Detroit," I said.

"No, you live on Grosse Ile," James said with a big grin, exposing a shiny gold tooth. "Look here, man, I don't care where you live. Live in China, for all I care. In fact, I'm impressed that you live on Grosse Ile. It's a nice place. I live in the suburbs too, but there is nobody trying to get me fired like they're trying to get you fired."

"Who's trying to get me fired?" I asked.

"Your own people, that's who! We had a meeting with a union executive board member complaining about you guys wasting all the union's time and money on eliminating residency, and he said it's only Dombrowski pushing for the residency bill because he lives on Grosse Ile!"

I was in shock at what James had said. What James had told me, if true, would mean that a union executive board member had sold me out and was trying to get me fired! What about my family? How would I support them? What kind of person would do something like that? Was he that afraid of these guys that he would sell me out to get the heat off him? At eight o'clock sharp the next morning, a furious me was in that executive board member's office, looking for blood.

"I swear to you, James is lying!" he told me.

I didn't really believe him. I found out later that he did have a meeting with some anti-residency members, including James. But what could I do? He was an executive board member with the hammer, and if he did what he did, what else was he capable of? I didn't want to lose my job.

"All right," I said, "but if I ever get fired, I sure wouldn't want to be you!" That was a threat that I meant for I was always worried about getting fired for residency. Now I knew that he would be worried, too. We firefighters have an unwritten code in Detroit—death to any man who takes our job or our pension.

CHAPTER 28

1993

The year 1993 started off with a bang for me. I was off on New Year's Day. The next day, I worked, and I got my fourth department citation. It was early afternoon, and I had just laid down for a nap. New Year's Day was a tough one. I was at a Rose Bowl party, and I really needed my nap.

I was awakened by the alert, "Box alarm, Luther Street." I slid down the pole, jumped on Engine 33, and we were off. When we pulled up to the address, I saw we had a two-story dwelling with the first floor going, and Engine 48 was stretching line.

As I headed to the fire, a neighbor stopped me and said that a woman and her son Chucky were still inside up on the second floor. Two other firefighters, Tim McHale and David Muering, and I went up the front stairway through the smoke and heat to find them.

The fire hadn't reached the second floor yet, but the smoke and heat had. We crawled around, looking for Chucky and his mom. We found the mom, and then through the smoke, I noticed what looked like a little kid sitting on a couch. We were looking for an adult; nobody said anything about a little kid.

I didn't know if this was a real child or some doll. I shined my flashlight in his face and literally freaked out. The child had a mustache. I was still sleepy, and I didn't know if I was imagining this. I just froze. Tim crawled up and looked at the strange sight for a moment, and then he grabbed him and headed for the porch doorway.

Ladder 13 had put a ladder up and took them both from us and brought them down to the waiting EMS. I pulled off my mask and yelled to Tim, "What the hell was that?"

"I guess that's Chucky," said a laughing Tim.

It turned out that Chucky was a little person or a dwarf. Nobody told us. They gave us citations for that rescue. But if I live to a hundred, I'll never forget that little face with a mustache. I never got back to sleep that afternoon.

I was working very hard on the residency bill. A week didn't go by that I wasn't up in Lansing, meeting with legislators. I was there so often that a lobbyist firm offered me a job. I almost took it. Also, on weekends I was organizing field trips to different legislative districts.

We would get thirty or forty firemen and go door-to-door in a legislative district, trying to get the voters to contact their legislator to support our bill. They would usually ask us why their representative wasn't for our bill. We had a great response, "He doesn't want to get Mayor Young angry." Nothing riled outstate voters more than the name Coleman Young, Detroit's famous mayor.

The City was really after me for residency. Phoenix (the association of black firefighters) warned me that I was number one on the list to be fired for residency violations, and they were right. Every night, City investigators would come around for a bed check. After a while, I couldn't fall asleep until I saw them there.

I would lie in bed with the curtain open, like a kid at Christmas waiting for Santa Claus, except I was waiting for a private investigator that the city hired to fire me. A woman in a white Ford Escort was the main investigator on my case. She would pull up between twelve and one. Sometimes we would wave to each other.

Back at the suburban house, it wasn't much better. Whenever I was on the island (that is what we call Grosse Ile), I would have a regular routine. The garage door must always be closed. Never sit on the front porch, back deck only. My neighbors knew that if anyone came by asking about me that it was a city residency investigator, no matter who they said they were.

My kids all had a routine that they followed. Rule 1, never tell anyone that I'm a Detroit firefighter. Rule 2, if they found out, say "My dad lives in Detroit." It was almost like we were living in a communist country. I always watched my back. I drove my car with one eye in the rearview mirror. God help anyone who mistakenly knocked on my front door.

One afternoon, I was at my Detroit home, doing some landscape work. I had parked my car in the back alley instead of in front, where I usually parked it. I finished my work and was driving out of the alley and decided to swing by the front of my house.

I stopped in front to admire my work, and parked right there in front was a residency investigator. He didn't notice me at first because he was busy writing his report. He looked up and saw me right there next to him. His eyes got as big as baseballs. He dropped his clipboard, put his car in drive, and sped out of there.

For some reason, this time I went ballistic. I was sick of this crap. I spun my car around and chased him. He turned left onto Michigan Avenue, squealing his tires, driving like a madman. I was right behind him. We were passing cars and changing lanes, like a bank robber with a cop in pursuit.

I chased him down Michigan Avenue for a few crazy miles, then I thought to myself, *this is silly*, and I slowed down and pulled into a coffee shop, but not before I got his license number.

I had one of my cop friends run the plate. I found out that he lived in a suburb, which happened to be right on my way to the island. I started a new routine. Every morning on my way to the island, I would stop, get a coffee and a morning paper, and then park in front of his house for an hour while reading my paper.

Sometimes I would see the curtains open as someone inside peeked out. *How do you like it?* I wondered. *How do you like people spying on you?* I knew that this was his job, and maybe he didn't like it any better than I did. Nobody likes to get spied on, not in America. I continued this for a month and a half. I think he got the message. They never did fire me.

But all this residency stuff was really taking a toll on me. I was worried all the time. My hair was turning gray, and my neck had permanent kinks from looking over my shoulder. I knew that a big part of my problem was due to me being a union director.

I had been a director for four terms and loved it. I won every time I ran. I was fortunate in having the members' support. It was remarkable all that we had accomplished during my tenure—the residency bill, the convention, the new safety gear, saving many jobs. I could go on and on. I knew that I was pretty good at what I did, but I was getting too stressed out. I had to move on. So in 1993, sadly, I didn't seek reelection to the union board.

I knew that I would miss working for the union, a cause that I believe in to this day. Do not attack unions in my presence. I loved helping firemen out with their problems. I enjoyed arguing at the meetings and writing my monthly columns for the magazine. Leaving was sad, but I did have two good things that I could console myself with: it's always better to leave too early than to leave too late, and I was about to make lieutenant.

CHAPTER 29

1994

In 1994, the International Association of Fire Fighters held their convention in Detroit. It was the convention that I had worked very hard to help bring to our City. I no longer was a director, just a member. I was surprised that I wasn't invited or even asked to help out. The sad truth is when you're out, you're out, and the guys in figure they don't need advice from you.

But I had a lot of friends from other locals who were coming to town that I wanted to see, so I went to the opening reception. It was held at the ballroom of the Renaissance Center, our big riverfront hotel. It was a nice reception with a bunch of old cars on display. To my surprise, there were no hospitality rooms—rooms paid for by different vendors passing out free drinks and favors, a staple of every convention.

I asked a union official why there weren't any hospitality rooms, and he said, "The hotel won't let us have any."

"You rented the whole hotel. You own this place. Don't let them tell you that you can't have hospitality rooms. It's part of every convention!" I said.

I was disappointed. Firefighters from all over America were coming to Detroit at our request, and we didn't have hospitality rooms. Every firefighter's convention I have ever attended was filled with hospitality rooms, but not here.

"What is this supposed to be, some drunken soiree?" he asked.

"Yep, that's exactly what conventions are!" I said.

But I couldn't blame him. He wasn't really a partyer like me. Perhaps it was my fault. Maybe I should have stayed on another term to see this thing through. Big locals like Detroit get credit cards or expense checks to cover their expenses at conventions. But the little locals come on their own expense and depend on the free stuff at hospitality rooms. Plus hospitality rooms are a lot of fun. It was the best place to meet different firefighters and learn about new products and new ideas.

I did the best I could to make up for it. The next couple of nights, I came down in my minivan, went into the hotel lobby, loaded as many out-of-town firefighters as I could into my minivan, and took them barhopping on my dime.

Detroit has some great old bars downtown: Casey's, Nancy Whiskey's, and the Soup Kitchen, just to name a few. They all had a great time. For the next month, my mailbox was filled with thank-you notes, T-shirts, and invites from all over America.

One friend from the West Coast who came to town was Paul Harvery, who was the president of the Seattle Firefighters Union. Over the years, he had heard so much about Detroit from me that he had to see it for himself. Next day that I was working, I invited him to come to Engine 33 and ride our rig.

Seattle was probably the exact opposite of Detroit. It was a rich and modern city. Microsoft and Boeing both headquartered there. The West Coast and the East Coast are where the richest and best-equipped fire departments are. Cities like New York, Boston, Los Angeles, San Francisco, and Seattle lead the way in innovative firefighting, wages, equipment, and just general conditions. Lucky guys!

It wasn't always that way. Detroit and most of the northern cities, back in the old manufacturing days, were cutting edge, just like the two coasts are now. Detroit was rated the best fire department in the United States in the early fifties. But now that manufacturing and the money had left us, many of the old Rust Belt cities, with the exception of Chicago, were second tier.

When Paul and his West Coast pals showed up, we didn't let them down. We had two of the rattiest rigs they ever saw. The engine's water tank leaked water so bad they had a hose running water into it continuously. The rig's compartment doors were rusted and tied shut with rope. We let them go through the compartments to marvel at our too-few tools and our one axe.

One axe became a running joke with my West Coast pals. We only carried one axe on our rigs, and at the time, we had no power saws. We would have two guys on a roof sharing an axe. None of them could believe an American city would have fire trucks with only one axe. Welcome to Detroit.

We took the guys around our district, showing them all our burnt-out buildings. They marveled at our potholed streets and the hundreds of fire hydrants with Out of Service tags on them. Hydrants that were so old, some from as far back as the 1860s, and so overused that they were falling apart. Often, we had to go a couple of blocks from the fire before we can find a working hydrant.

We caught a dwelling fire, giving them a chance to see us in action. They saw firsthand how fast we were extinguishing a dwelling fire and how, without orders, everyone jumped off the rig and went right to work. That's experience that comes from day after day of fighting fires.

After their tour, Paul said, "You guys have some of the worst equipment I've ever seen, but you make up for it with great firefighting," It was a very nice compliment from my West Coast pal.

Engine 33 was one of those fire stations where someone was always getting in trouble. So I wasn't completely surprised as I arrived for work one morning and found the place surrounded by police cars and fire-chief cars. I parked my car and carefully walked in the back door.

Once inside, I was stunned to learn that an air tank blew up and took half the rig with it. Luckily, no one was killed or injured. I went to inspect the damage. The rig was surrounded by yellow crime-scene tape. I stepped over, and as soon as I did, a hand grabbed me by the collar and said, "See that yellow tape? You don't step over it!"

I recognized the person. He was an arson investigator. Now I was a lieutenant and in charge of Engine 33. The rig blew up, but according to him, I still wasn't allowed to enter and inspect my rig.

The guys explained to me that they had returned from a fire at 5:00 a.m., put new air tanks in their harnesses, and had gone upstairs to sleep. A few minutes later, the whole enginehouse shook with a loud explosion. They all ran downstairs and found the rig blown up. The back part of the cab, where the firefighters rode, was ripped apart. They immediately called Central and went out of service. The bomb squad came out and determined that an air tank had blown up and caused all the damage. Unbelievable!

There was more bad news. The air tank that blew up was one of the brand-new aluminum tanks the City had just bought us. We had fought for years to get the new aluminum tanks. We had been wearing the old steel tanks that weighed around thirty pounds and felt like you were carrying two bowling balls on your back. The new aluminum tanks, which weighed half as much, were the best things for firemen since air tanks were invented.

The company that made the tanks was notified of what happened. They notified every fire department in the United States who bought the new tanks to take them out of service immediately. We were then notified that the CEO and a crew of engineers were flying in the company jet to personally inspect the damaged tank.

The chief of department kept me there to handle all the people who would be showing up. And they showed up nonstop, the air tank people, the state police, and other fire departments. Everyone was trying to figure out how this air tank blew up. Were the new aluminum air tanks defective, or was the tank somehow damaged?

Early that evening, they figured it out. At the last fire they had, just before the tank blew up, someone had removed his air harness and laid it on the street to help with a roof rescue. A second engine pulling up to the scene didn't see the air tank and ran over it. When the firefighter picked up his damaged harness, he had no idea what had happened to it. When they returned, he switched harnesses and unknowingly put the damaged air tank into a new harness and put it back on the rig. The damaged harness was then placed along the wall with all the other broken equipment, ready to be taken to the shop next day.

I knew what was going to happen next. The department was pissed off. They had caused a large company a lot of trouble. Someone was going to pay for this. The department figured there was some kind of a conspiracy going on, and the key to the conspiracy was that damaged air harness, which had now disappeared.

Around midnight, it was my turn to be harassed. Two arson investigators, one was the same one who grabbed me earlier by the collar, came in to talk to me. They both had their Dick Tracy looks on their faces, so I knew that I was in for some fun.

"Now I want you to tell us who took that harness. Do not lie to us. Think about what you're going to say because we are writing everything down, and it will be held against you. You could even go to jail," he said.

"When I came in this morning, there was yellow tape surrounding the rig," I told him. "I stepped over it, and you grabbed me by the collar and told me that you were in charge and that I could not enter the scene. So the only person who could have removed that harness was you or someone you allowed in there. If you want me to, I will write it all down and sign it." They both just stared at me then got up and left.

Later, they finally did find the damaged air harness. It was at the repair shop, waiting to be repaired just like it should have been. The city gave up on trying to hang someone. But the best news was that there was nothing wrong with our light new aluminum air tanks. Just don't run them over.

CHAPTER 30

Fire poles, those shiny brass poles that firemen slide down on, have been in fire stations ever since the invention of fire stations. Bedrooms, or dorm rooms, as we called them, were upstairs and the apparatus room, where we kept the fire trucks, was downstairs. To get from the dorm to the apparatus room, you slid down the pole.

Fire poles were a symbol of firefighting. When you first came on the job, you were taught how to slide down the pole. Whenever friends or family visited, the first thing they wanted to see was you sliding down the pole. And we loved to show people. Every Saturday morning, we cleaned and shined the poles with brass cleaner.

Taking the stairs on night runs was unheard of because sliding down the pole was so much faster. You would never make the rig running down the stairs. But that began to change when we got air conditioners. Upstairs, where the fire poles came through the floor, you had spring loaded doors. The first person would pop the doors, and everyone would slide down, leaving the pole hole doors open until you returned. All the hot air would rise up into the dorm through the open pole hole, and you would return to a hot dorm.

So with the AC running on hot days, we all started taking the stairs. Pretty soon this caught on, and before you knew it, everybody was using the stairs. We still cherished our traditional fire poles, and we still slid down them for visitors and when the AC wasn't on.

The one time that firemen didn't stop using the poles was in the morning at the start of their shift. It seemed that guys often came to work and the first thing they did was slide down the pole and injure themselves. This happened a lot on the days following baseball and basketball tournaments.

Many injury letters started out with the words "While sliding the pole at 0735 hours, I twisted my knee" or "I twisted my ankle." In fact, there were so many injuries while sliding down the pole at seven thirty in the morning that the Michigan Department of Safety got involved. Then somebody determined that the poles were dangerous and must be removed.

This became a big argument with firefighters who loved the poles and wanted to keep them. They were a symbol of Detroit firefighting, just like the red trucks and our traditional helmets.

In the 1990s, all the fire poles disappeared from the fire stations. First we heard that the City was coming around and removing the fire poles. Next we heard that they were going to sell them all to some scrapper. We had to make a choice. We wanted to keep our poles, but we knew if the City wanted them, they were as good as gone.

It all happened quickly one day. The guys voted to take the fire poles down. I voted no, hoping that some way we could save them, but I was outvoted. They decided to cut them up, and everyone who wanted a piece could have one.

"You got two choices, have a piece of the fire pole or not. But nevertheless, we're taking them down."

"Well, I guess I'll have a piece then," I said.

So there they went, 150 years of history sadly gone in one day. You can still see fire poles. They are in hundreds of personal fire museums, where they are meticulously maintained, in smaller sizes, of course. The museums are in firefighters' basements everywhere, where the fire poles, along with all the other fire department knickknacks we have accumulated over the years, are proudly displayed.

On May 25, 1995, a Detroit police officer, Jerry Philpot, was shot and killed in the alley right across the street from Engine 33's quarters, where I was running at the time. Two of the local gangs were having a gun battle in the alley. The police officer was caught in the cross fire as he entered the alley.

The cops knew who the shooter was, and a massive manhunt was on. They searched all over town for him. It was the number one story on the news. Cops and news reporters were all over the neighborhood.

On a sunny Saturday morning, three of us were standing in front of quarters, listening to Jimmy, a Detroit cop who patrolled the streets in our area. Jimmy told us about the manhunt going on, then he handed us a flyer with the shooter's picture on it. Just as we were looking at the picture on the flyer, a cab pulled up, and the shooter got out and walked into the house right next door. I pointed to the guy and said, "Jimmy, there he is!" The shooter looked over at us and walked in.

Damn, what an exciting moment! I thought. Here's the guy that the whole City is looking for, public enemy 1, and here's Jimmy with a chance to make a big name for himself. Jimmy was a motorman. Motormen are the only Detroit cops who ride all alone. They spend all day writing speeding tickets. They are sometimes called the Barney Fifes of the precinct.

"Well, what are you going to do, Jimmy? He's in there. Go get him!" we said.

Just then, a shiny black Crown Vic pulled up, and two guys jumped out with wicked-looking shotguns, then they ran up to Jimmy and shouted, "FBI. We just followed that scumbag here. We're going in the front door to get him. You cover the back door."

Jimmy, with his pistol in hand, ran around the back, and I followed him. I figured if the guy saw the two badass FBI guys coming in the front and Jimmy out back, back would be the direction he would head. But it never happened; the bad guy surrendered without a fight.

Then a funny thing happened. As they walked the handcuffed bad guy to a police car, he stopped and stared right at me with one of those if-looks-could-kill stares. As he stood there staring, all the firemen moved away from me. Later that day, the TV news reported that he was caught by a tip from a fireman.

Well, it really took off from there. The gangs now had somebody to blame for their member's capture. The word went out in the neighborhood that they were going to get the fireman who snitched. Now they had something new to spray-paint on the walls: threats to the firemen at the Lawndale and Lafayette fire station!

Some of the guys pointed out that it was me that they were after. "Look," I told them, "they couldn't tell one of us from the other, so if the shit comes down, it could be anyone of us who gets it."

Now we couldn't care less about their threats. We knew that they were just a bunch of punks, and we were very glad that they got the cop killer. But the media played up the story about how the gangs were after the firemen at Engine 33.

The city got involved and decided to have a policeman move in with us 24-7. At first it was okay. He or she, depending on the day, just sat around, watching TV and eating our food. It was a lot like having some relative move in. But after a while, it started to get old. As Benjamin Franklin once said, "Fish and guests start to smell after three days." I agree.

After a few weeks, things began to die down. The gang threats stopped, and our police guests finally left. They were probably sick of us too. Things went back to normal. I just wonder if in thirty years' time, when he gets out of prison, they're going to need those cops back.

CHAPTER 31

1996

In 1996, I was promoted to senior lieutenant and was transferred to Ladder 27. Senior lieutenant is the lowliest promotion because you don't get a pay raise or a real promotion, just a transfer, usually from some place that you were happy to run at to a place that you won't be.

Up until then, most of my career had been spent in southwest Detroit, mainly in the Seventh Battalion. Now I would be running in northwest Detroit. The fire department was somewhat segregated by members' choice. Firefighters in the southwest and the east side battalions of the City were mostly white; most of the black firefighters ran in the northern and northwest battalions. Why different groups went to where they went, I have no idea; it's just the way it was.

Running in northwest Detroit or on the line, as we called it, would be a new experience for me. Ladder 27 was a double house with a battalion chief. I really had no complaints. Everyone was friendly and respectful. The place was clean, the chow was good, and the fires went out. In fact, in some ways, it was easier running there than back in the Seventh with all my buddies.

One day, something happened to me that had never happened before. It surprised the hell out of me. We were coming back from a run, and it was a hot afternoon during rush hour. Ladder 27 is located on Joy Road and the Southfield Freeway. We were creeping along the Southfield Service Drive and parked along the service drive, I noticed, was a group of men with a truck, and they were loading fence in the back.

There is a big vacant complex on this corner called Herman Gardens. Herman Gardens was a housing project built during the World War II to help house all the workers who were moving to Detroit for jobs in the defense plants. The project fell into disrepair and was torn down a few years ago. All that was left was a half-mile-wide, vacant field surrounded by a decorative wrought iron fence. Now a group of men were cutting down the fence and loading it into a truck.

I told my driver to stop the rig. I looked at the men and asked, "What are you doing?"

"We're taking the fence down," one of them replied.

"Are you guys stealing the fence?" I asked.

They just looked at me with a surprised look on their faces. I figured, by the look that they gave me, they were stealing the fence. Our fire station was located right across the street. As we were backing in, I jumped out of the rig and called the police. It was a miracle, but within a couple of minutes, a cop car was on the scene and had all of them sitting handcuffed on the service drive. I was pretty happy that they were arrested, but I was very surprised at what happened next.

The guys were all upset at what I did. "Why did you do that, Lieutenant? They know that it's us who turned them in, and now they're going to get us!" they said.

I couldn't believe what I was hearing. These guys were stealing the fence right in front of us in broad daylight, and the firemen were mad at me for turning them in. Now I knew that we were vulnerable. Our cars sat out back unprotected, and the engine houses got robbed all the time. Maybe they would get us. But so what? Right is right. I immediately called for roll call and lined everyone up on the apparatus floor.

"Listen," I told them, "every one of you took an oath when you became a fireman to save lives and to protect property. Whenever you see a crime being committed, you have to act. You took an oath, and they gave you a badge to protect this city. If we don't hold up law and order, then who will? I don't care what happens to us, but to let them get away with it would have made us just as bad as them."

I was upset. Most of the firemen on duty that afternoon were younger and minorities. I was an older white guy who they probably thought lived in the suburbs. I was often told that us white suburbanites didn't care about the City and just took a paycheck and then headed back to the suburbs. After that day, I decided that no one would ever make that statement to me again.

Good news came to the firemen at the Joy Road station. The city was going to remodel our old fire station. One morning, some guy showed up wearing a nice suit with a clipboard in his hand and said, "I'm from the company that's going to remodel this fire station. What do you fellas need done?"

We rattled off everything that was important to us. "Air-conditioning in the dorm. Fix the potholes and fence in the back parking lot, and how about replacing the gutters and painting the exterior trim that looked so bad?"

He told us that they would fix everything, plus they would remodel the kitchen and the bathrooms, install new lighting, and fix up the exterior with badly needed paint and new gutters. He then went out front and put up a sign that said we were being remodeled by his company.

We were all excited by this good news. The city rarely ever puts a dime in these old barns, but now that was changing, we thought. That good thought didn't last very long. Day by day our new friend stopped by, and each time he sadly told us another thing they wouldn't be able to do. The AC was gone, the parking lot was gone, and before long, the only things they were going to do were the kitchen and new sinks upstairs.

There was nothing wrong with our old sinks; in fact, we liked them. They were original sinks they had installed back when they built the station in the 1920s. I figured they planned to replace them with some cheap new ones and haul our classic old porcelain sinks to the northern suburbs.

When it came time to do our kitchen was when I really got upset. They were going to cover our floor with some cheap asphalt tile, the stuff people used to put in their basements. That tile wouldn't last a year here.

I could only imagine the larceny that must be going on. How much was the City paying for this shoddy so-called remodeling job? I wondered. I finally had enough, and I told him, "If you lay one piece of that cheap asphalt tile here, I will go to the council, to the media, or to whoever will listen and let them know what's going on here!"

My friend with the clipboard wasn't smiling anymore. He just glared at me. But they never did lay that cheap tile. The next day, they brought in some nice ceramic stuff that's still wearing very well. I took some pride in that floor whenever I stopped back there.

I can only imagine all the thieves, con-men, and crooked politicians that take advantage of our fair City. There are few people worse than con-men like that. Occasionally, one will go to jail. It happens often in this town, but not enough. If it was up to me, I wouldn't send them to jail. I would hang them from trees or from the broken gutters that they never replaced.

CHAPTER 32

The transfer openings came out, and there was an opening for a senior lieutenant at Engine 37 back in Southwest Detroit, my old hood. I put in a request and was soon on my way back. My wife thought I was crazy going back to the Seventh, and I must admit, my year out on the line at Ladder 27 was practically trouble-free.

But trouble is what I'm used to, and I figured it would be waiting for me with open arms. For starters, they moved Engine 37 from the Seventh Battalion to the Second Battalion. It made no sense. We would never run with Chief 2, but we were assigned to his domain. Because we were in a different area, far from his quarters, we would be the first company he would short to three men even though we were a busy single house.

My daily crew usually consisted of three men, an FEO named Charlie, who I didn't get along with, a trial man, and myself. This would be my day. I would get there in the morning, do the paperwork, make a pot of soup, if there was anything in the refrigerator to make soup with, while the FEO cleaned and checked the rig and the trial man cleaned the engine house.

Then we all jumped in the rig, delivered the daily mail to the chief, got fuel, went to the shop, did our hydrants, then went grocery shopping at E & L, a market in Mexican Town. I returned, cooked lunch, and went up and tried to take an afternoon nap.

After my nap, I came down, cooked the second meal, and waited for the runs to come in, and they did, all night long. Back then, we were riding short, three men on the rigs, and the chiefs always called for a fourth engine, which usually was us. We covered the entire southwest side of Detroit.

Back at quarters, if by chance I had a slow night, sleep would still be out of the question. The Highwaymen Motorcycle Club had a clubhouse not far away and would run all night long, up and down Central with their straight-piped Harleys. The EMS had their office right below and would be chattering between runs all night long.

The EMS that ran out of there was probably the friendliest EMS crew in the city. At most fire stations, the firefighters and the EMS did not get along and rarely spoke to each other. The hostility between firemen and EMS techs went back to the early seventies, when the EMS first started. The techs were mostly young Vietnam-era medics hired by the City to do the medical runs. They put them in our fire stations with their own officers and their own set of rules. This caused huge resentment between the two groups that still goes on in many stations but not at Engine 37's quarters.

The EMS was a welcomed friendship, and we had enjoyable conversations whenever they were in quarters. But the EMS was usually on the road, going from run to run. They worked a twelve-hour shift because they were too busy to run a twenty-four-hour shift. They changed shifts at 7:00 a.m. and 7:00 p.m. More times than not, they would switch crews in front of quarters.

The EMS rig would pull up, lights and sirens on, for they were on a run. The old crew would hop out, the new crew would hop in, and then they would continue on their run. They had to do it this way or continue running all over the city for a couple more hours. Good luck collecting any overtime.

We called ourselves the junkyard dogs because we were surrounded by junkyards and railroad tracks. One night, we responded to a car wreck on the tracks. The police pulled up right when we did. We had a pizza-delivery vehicle that was broadsided by a car that was drag racing down John Kronk. He smashed the pizza driver's car up onto the railroad tracks.

The police called their dispatch and told them to shut the tracks down. The pizza driver was unconscious and trapped in his vehicle. We called for a squad with the Jaws of Life, but none was available. We pulled out our bars and went to work to free the driver.

As we were working to free him, we heard the horn from the train. We kept working because we thought that the tracks were closed. The horn was growing louder and louder, then to our horror, the train came around the bend. It was the Amtrak train going full throttle right on the tracks that we were on!

The words "Jump for your life" will never have a bigger meaning for me than they did at that moment. We all jumped off the car just a moment before impact. The train hit the car; it went flying in the air for an unforgettable moment of terror. The car came down a few feet off the tracks as the Amtrak train came to a screeching halt a block down the tracks.

We all got back on our feet, checked if everyone was all right, and then ran to the wreck. The poor pizza driver was trapped in it all this time. Luckily, we had put a cervical collar on him, and the train hit the rear portion of his vehicle. He didn't look any worse than before.

We went back to work to free him. We carefully pulled him out of the wreck and handed him over to the waiting EMS. They hauled him to Receiving, and we headed back to Engine 37. Believe it or not, the driver managed to pull through. Amazing!

Summertime is hydrant time in Detroit. People all over the city illegally turn fire hydrants on so they can run through them and cool off. After they are finished playing in the water, they call us to turn them off. We usually wait until we have three or four to turn off before we go out, so that we're not constantly running to turn off hydrants.

We were out one hot afternoon, turning off hydrants on Norman Street with our usual crew of three: the FEO, the trial man, and me. The trial man jumped off the rig to shut the fire hydrant off and yelled, "Lieutenant, it's broke."

I got out of the rig to inspect it, and yep, they broke it. I looked down east of the street and noticed that the hydrant had a yellow Out of Service tag on it. I looked back west, and that hydrant was also out of service. "Great," I said, "every hydrant on the street is out of service."

Standing there, watching us, was a lady and her little girl. She was looking at us and laughing. Unfortunately for me, I blew up. "You think this is funny!" I yelled. "Look, every hydrant on the street is broken, and we can't get any water, and with all the fires we have around here, your house could burn down before we could get any water!"

My FEO got on the rig PA and started doing some type of rap, saying, "We got no water and y'all going to burn up." We put a tag on the hydrant and headed back to 37. The next morning, I was awakened by a call from the senior chief.

"Lieutenant Dombrowski, did you shut off a hydrant on Norman Street yesterday?"

"Yes, sir," I told him.

"Did anything bad happen?"

"No, not really," I said.

"Well, somebody from the mayor's office has called. You better get over there and see if you can straighten it out."

But I knew there would be no straightening it out. These folks watch enough daytime TV to know that firemen can't say anything anymore. The good people on Norman Street were hoping they hit pay dirt. They were busy calling anyone who would listen. They said they couldn't sleep, couldn't eat, and their kids were having nightmares. It was just horrible what those firemen said!

The deputy chief called me at home and said, "Look, I can understand what happened, but if this becomes a big story on the news, someone's got to hang, and that someone will probably be you. If it blows over, don't worry about it."

Well, I had a couple of worried days, but it blew over. There was a big murder, and another politician got in trouble, and soon every one forgot about the fireman giving kids nightmares on Norman Street.

CHAPTER 33

The city sent us another trial man, a young kid named Louie. It was his first day at the engine house; he was fresh from the academy. I showed him around quarters, and then I had him go through the rig. Lastly, I told him all the usual stuff, including what I expected of him at fires.

"Never give up the line, stay busy, stick with me, and if we're lucky, we'll all make it through the day," I said. Louie seemed friendly and eager and, like most new trial men on their first day, a little nervous.

After the work at quarters was finished, we went out on the road to drop off the mail and to hit all our other stops. We were parked in front of a chiropractor's office that our FEO was visiting when a still alarm (small fire) came over the radio. I hit the horn, and he ran out and jumped in the rig, and we were off on our trial man's first run.

The run was for a dwelling on Central, just a few blocks from our location. As we got close, I could see heavy smoke coming from the rear of the dwelling. It was going! We had a burning story-and-a-half frame bungalow with a hip roof. We pulled up. I told Louie to stretch the one-and-a-half-inch line, and I called Central for the box.

Louie grabbed the bundle, and as I helped him, he stretched it to the front porch. I told him, "Break the bundle, put your mask on, and wait for me. Don't move from this spot!"

I went into the dwelling for a quick look-see to plan our attack strategy. It was as clear as day. I walked to the back of the home, and there was not a bit of smoke downstairs. When I got to the rear of the dwelling, I found the fire. It was going pretty good up the back stairway and up to the attic, which was also starting to take off.

I went back through the house to the outside front porch, where my trial man was waiting for me with the now-charged one-and-a-half-inch line. I had just reached him when—*bam*—the whole house blew up and collapsed in an explosion. It blew me and Louie right off the porch!

I got up and looked over to Louie.

"You okay?" I asked.

"Yes, Lieutenant, I'm all right," Louie said.

The second story had collapsed and buried itself into the first floor. The whole dwelling was instantly turned into a huge pile of burning wood. Had we been in that home a few moments earlier, we would have both been toast.

The rest of the companies from the box were arriving on the scene and started to attack the fire. Louie and I picked ourselves up and joined in. It was just a big bonfire now that would need a lot of overhauling.

After the fire was out, the line was picked up, and we were leaving, Louie said, "Wait a second, Lieutenant. I left my eyeglasses back there on the porch."

"Oh no," I said, "Louie, you took your glasses off and left them on the porch. You can't ever do that. That house just collapsed and burnt down, and you have zero chance of finding them in one piece."

I walked back with him, and to my surprise, there they were, right where he left them, sitting among the ruins without a scratch on them. I couldn't believe it. No one had stepped on them. Louie picked them up, blew the dust off, and put them on his smiling face.

"Three hours on the job. You survive a house collapse, and you leave your glasses on the porch and find them unbroken. I think you're going to have a lucky career," I told him.

Early one evening, Engine 37 responded alone to an auto fire a few blocks north of quarters. Right from the start, something didn't look right. It was a compact, late-model, dark blue Buick. The fire was out when we arrived, but the interior was burnt, lightly singed.

Inside the glove box were a couple packets of family pictures. They looked fresh from the local photo mat. We opened the trunk and found a couple of neatly tied bags of return pop bottles and cans and a child's car seat.

Now most of the car fires we get that involve newer cars are usually inside jobs for insurance—people trying to get out of a lease or a car they can't sell. But this was strange; nobody leaves family pictures or a child's car seat.

I looked further, and I found some paperwork showing ownership to a family from Taylor, a downriver suburb. A civilian who was standing there, watching us, let me use his phone. I tried calling the owner with no luck.

We returned to quarters. As I was filling out the fire report, the local news was on, and the anchorman was reporting that a car had been hijacked in the city of Taylor, and a two-year-old boy had been shot in the head. I wondered if this car fire could be the hijacked car, so I called the Taylor police.

"We don't like giving out any information over the phone," the Taylor cop told me.

"Could you at least tell me what kind of car you're looking for?" I asked.

"A compact, dark blue Buick."

"Stop right there. I've got it!" I told him.

A few minutes later, the engine house door burst in, and what seemed like the entire Taylor Police Department came charging in.

"Where is it?" they yelled. I told them where the car was, and off they went.

The next morning, I was still feeling pretty good about what I did, and I called the Taylor Police to see if they wanted me to come in and make a report.

"No, that's okay. We got the kid, and we don't need any report from you," he told me.

"Well, you want to take my name and number in case anything comes up and you need to get a hold of me?" I asked.

"No, we don't need your name or number," he said.

I was a little surprised and disappointed at this. I thought I helped these cops out, and at least they could humor me and take my number. But they didn't want it, so I let it go and forgot all about it.

A year later, I was at the engine house, nursing a toothache, when I got a call from the Taylor Police.

"Lieutenant Dombrowski, we need you to come downtown to court tomorrow at 10:00 a.m. and testify in that car hijacking."

"I got a dentist appointment at ten," I told him.

"Not anymore," he said.

"No, I got a dentist appointment at ten tomorrow morning, and that's where I'll be. I will come to court afterward. That's the best I can do. Besides, when this happened, you guys didn't even want my phone number. You call me a year later, at the last moment, and I'm supposed to just drop everything? I got a toothache."

We agreed that I would come right after my dentist appointment. When I got to the courthouse, they put me in a little room off the side of the courtroom with a couple of Taylor cops.

"Is there anything that you guys want to tell me? After all, it's been over a year."

"No, it's pretty open-and-shut. The kid did it, no doubt," the cops said.

When they called me in to testify, I was surprised to see the lawyer, who I'll call Detroit's own Johnny Cochran, defending the kid. Detroit Johnny was a well-known criminal defense attorney. It seems that every day Johnny is on the five o'clock news, getting some murderer or drug dealer acquitted for his crimes.

Sitting up front next to Johnny was the defendant with a respectable haircut and wearing a nice new suit. He looked more like a student at one of those fancy prep schools north of the city than a gang-banging, carjacking shooter of a two-year-old.

As I sat in the witness chair, Detroit Johnny approached me with that practiced look of concerned wisdom on his face. First, he asked me all about myself and my career and how long I'd been a firefighter. Then he handed me a stack of photos and asked me to identify them.

The photos were all of the car, the blue Buick with the lightly burned interior and the trunk with the pop bottles and the child's car seat.

"Is there anything there that you don't recognize or is out of order?" he asked.

"No, sir," I said.

"All right, now let me show you a couple more pictures."

This time I gasped as I looked at them. Here were pictures of stuff I did not remember. There was a picture of a white Ivory dish detergent bottle laying on a burnt car seat without a smudge on it and a picture of a newspaper rolled into a torch lying on top of the return bottles.

"Were those items there?" Johnny asked.

Now I was 90 percent sure that they weren't there, but I knew something was going on here, and the fact that Johnny was showing them to me with a gleam in his eyes meant that he had some scheme going.

I looked up and said, "I don't remember seeing them."

"Yes or no. Were they there?" he yelled.

"As I said, I don't remember seeing them there."

It had been over a year, and I never reviewed the case with the cops or a prosecutor, but Johnny didn't seem to care. He spent the next half hour asking me over and over whether I saw that stuff in those pictures. He then went on to ask what kind of firefighter I was not to remember a torch and a plastic bottle filled with an accelerant.

When he finished with me, one thing everyone in the courtroom could agree with was that I was the most incompetent firefighter in America. As I left the courtroom, I asked the cops what the heck was going on. They just said they didn't know. The kid was acquitted in two hours.

Later, I was at work, telling the story to an arson investigator. They are in court all the time, and they know all the tricks. "The lawyer probably put them there," he told me.

"Sure, he probably went to the police lot, found it open and unguarded, and put them there and took those pictures. As a witness, you have three things you can say. One, that they weren't there and then he says that the evidence was tampered with and must be dismissed. Two, you say that they were there and then he says you're lying because he put them there. Or three, you say you don't remember and he makes a fool out of you."

Well, I chose the third and was made to look like a fool. That's the American justice system.

CHAPTER 34

1999

December 12, 1999, was a date that I'll never forget. It was a chilly Thursday morning just a couple weeks before Christmas. I walked out to the mailbox and grabbed the morning *Free Press*. As I walked back, I scanned the headlines and read State Kills Residency Laws.

I didn't understand what I had just read at first. The state legislature clears out all the bills introduced during the year before they break for the holidays. And usually one of the bills that they throw out is the residency bill. This is an annual event that we're used to. It had been this way for nearly fourteen years.

Then something made me stop and reread it. "State kills residency laws! What!" Then I understood; they killed the law, not the bill. I couldn't believe it. After fourteen hard-fought years, they finally passed our bill, and we finally won. No more residency rules. We were now free to live where we wanted, just like every other American.

I ran in and called my wife, who was at work.

"Linda," I wailed into the phone, "you won't believe what happened. Residency just passed!"

"Yes, I heard it on the radio, driving into work this morning."

"What! Why didn't you call me?"

"I didn't want to wake you," she said.

"News like this, you can wake me up a hundred times for."

I later heard that a state senator named Loren Bennett, whose brother was a Detroit cop, was the legislator who convinced the governor to finally run the bill. Governor Engler was using the bill to keep the Detroit legislators in line. Many times when they threatened to fight one of his bills, he would threaten to run the residency bill, which was worse than death to most of the Detroit legislators.

Detroit had lost half of its population, close to a million people. People were leaving the city in herds. Cops and firemen were forced to stay because of the residency law. We were paid by city tax dollars, and our presence helped to stabilize some neighborhoods, or so they said. No Detroit politician wanted to see this rule change and lose us. Any Detroit politician not fighting for the residency laws would be DOA.

The story of how the residency bill was finally passed, as told to me, was this: Senator Bennett went to the governor's office with a group of senators and threatened to form a group and vote against the governor and his legislation if he didn't run the bill. The governor looked up and said, "Are you kidding?" Then he picked up the phone and called the committee chair and said, "This is John. Run the residency bill." That was it. Rarely in politics does something like that happen, especially for a group of cops and firemen with little money and little power.

The bill's signing date was December 22, just three days before Christmas, and what a Christmas present it would be.

Terry Chesney, secretary of the Michigan Professional Fire Fighters, called me up and invited me to the official governor's signing. "You started the bill, and you should be there," he said. I was happy to be invited by the state even though my local union didn't invite me. They must have forgotten.

I managed to get a chair right up front. The governor came in and said, "This bill is about freedom for those who put their lives on the line for us every day. It's about the freedom for our law enforcement officers and firefighters to choose where they want to live." Words well spoken.

I got a copy of the bill with the governor's signature and the pen that he used to sign it. I put them in a frame and hung it on a wall. It's one of my prized possessions after fourteen years of hard work and a great storybook ending.

February 6, 2001, I was promoted to captain and transferred to Engine 23 on Detroit's east side. I hadn't been to this engine house in twenty-five years; now I was going there as the captain. Engine 23 was a double house, and the other company running there was Squad 3.

Squad 3 and the west side's Squad 4 were Detroit's legendary, top-notch squad companies, kind of like our own SEAL teams. I had spent most of my time down in the Seventh Battalion, a more laid-back battalion. Now I would be in charge of a house of hotshots. I didn't know many of the firefighters there, and most of them probably didn't know me, so I was a little hesitant when I first entered.

But the guys couldn't have been better, and soon I felt right at home. They were some great firemen, and they were some great jokesters. It was an ordeal sitting at that dining room table every morning, listening to them verbally work over each other. They were good at it, and nothing was sacred. Movie stars say that the first seat on the old *Johnny Carson Show* was the hardest seat in the world to sit in. The second hardest might be a seat at the dining room table at Engine 23.

Engine 23 borders Hamtramck, an old Polish city. We would take the rig there to shop at the Polish meat markets and bakeries. The women working in these shops treated the guys like rock stars, especially Chuckie, who was their favorite. It was great for me. We would go in the bakery for bread, and they would load us down with donuts and cakes and angel wings. I think I gained ten pounds running there.

You can always tell a good fire station by where they send firemen's kids when they become firemen. When a fireman's kid gets on the job, the city usually sends him or her to a station that the dad requested. Engines 23, Engine 10, Engine 42 are always on that requested list. So being a captain at one of those fire stations means that you usually will have a trial man, and it's usually a fireman's kid.

My trial man was a kid I'll call Jason, a good kid whose dad and uncle were both firemen. One night we had a dwelling fire, and Jason and I climbed up on a porch overhang to enter the second-story window. The overhang collapsed and smashed down on the porch. We just rode it down. Luckily, nobody was on the porch when it collapsed.

They took us both to Detroit Receiving Hospital to get checked out. We were a little banged up but we were okay.

Afterward we were both sitting in front of Receiving Hospital, waiting for the squad to pick us up, when Jason's mother pulled up. Thirty years of firefighting and I've never seen a mother pick up her injured firefighter son, but this was a fireman's kid, and word somehow gets out to firemen's moms, even at six in the morning. Lucky, that Jason was okay.

"You want a ride back to quarters, Captain?" she asked.

"No, I'll just wait for the squad, but thanks anyway," I said.

After seven months of running at Engine 23, the transfer list came out, and I was getting booted. A captain with more seniority was pushing me out. To my surprise, a couple of the guys asked me to try to stay, and I would have liked to stay, but I didn't have enough seniority at the time. But luck was with me, and I got sent to another great spot, Engine 10 back in the Seventh, my old hood.

CHAPTER 35

2001

My first day as captain at my new quarters, Engine 10, was September 11, 2001, the day of infamy for every American firefighter. When I walked in that morning at seven, I was surprised to find out that I had to go to school for eight hours. The school was Weapons of Mass Destruction Counterterrorism School at Cobo Hall. It was taught by the US Army. Obviously, I had no idea of what was going to happen in just two hours or the irony of having this class on this day.

Our class consisted of a group of firefighters and police officers from Detroit and the surrounding suburbs. The instructors were an E7 from the army and a fire chief from Los Angeles, California.

About an hour into our class, a firefighter looked up from his pager and said, "A plane hit the World Trade Center."

"No, I think you're mistaken. It was the Empire State Building that got hit by a bomber back in the forties," I said.

Looking back at his pager, he said, "Nope, it was the World Trade Center, and a second plane just hit it."

It was that moment that everyone remembers where they were when they heard of the terrorist attack. The entire class jumped up and ran out of the room, looking for a TV. We found one down the hall, and like all Americans, we sat glued to it for the next couple of hours, watching the horror of it all. Beepers suddenly started going off, and police and fire commanders began contacting New York to see what assistance we could offer.

As I sat watching the Twin Towers burn out of control, I knew everyone on floors above the fire would die; there was no way to rescue them. Ladders only go up ten stories, and helicopters would be useless with all the smoke and wind. There was no stopping that fire, not when you have thousands of gallons of jet fuel burning. Watching people jump from those high floors would give me nightmares for weeks. The heat and smoke were so bad up there that they chose to jump to their deaths. We sat there watching in horror.

Firemen were entering the towers with hose lines over their shoulders and air tanks and axes in their arms, preparing to climb the stairs to fight the fire. I knew that it was crazy sending them up there; many would be killed. What a difficult decision for the chiefs on the scene. Firemen understand this is their job and this is that moment they always fear will come.

Then the towers came crashing down. For a moment, I thought that the world had just ended. We all sat and wondered how many people were just killed. How many firemen were just killed? We thought that maybe as many as twenty or thirty firemen were just killed. We had no idea that 343 New York firefighters would die that morning.

After a couple of hours, our instructors rounded us up for our lessons. We had to get back to why we were there now that the importance of our subject was multiplied by one hundred thousand. We spent the rest of the day working out different response scenarios to different types of terrorist attacks on high-rise buildings.

When I returned to my new quarters, they had satellite TV on, and we watched the local New York news channels the rest of the night, like all other Americans, not knowing what was going to happen next.

The department and the union contacted New York and got a list of stuff they needed. Firefighters immediately organized a caravan of off-duty firefighters and sent them to New York to help. They brought power saws and power tools and cases of spray paint to mark ways in and out of the Trade Center and to mark what areas had and what areas hadn't been searched. And like all the other fire departments across America, we stood on corners and filled our boots with donations to send to the FDNY.

A few days later, seven of us from Engine 10 put some time-off days together and headed to New York to help out. We contacted the New York Fire Department to see what they needed, and they said they needed us to go to funerals. New York City had lost 343 firefighters, and their families were starting to have the funerals.

At a fireman's funeral, hundreds or thousands of firefighters show up to pay their respect. We line up in a show of solidarity and give our fallen brother a final salute. It is a beautiful tribute and a final comfort for the family. But there would be too many funerals in New York. The sheer number was overwhelming. The surviving New York firemen couldn't attend them all. "Please bring your dress uniforms and attend funerals," they said. That's what we did.

For one week, every morning and afternoon, we attended different firefighters' funerals all over New York. How sad it was watching little kids excited at the spectacle of hundreds of uniformed firefighters and shiny red fire trucks, knowing that it was their father in that coffin, if there was a coffin. Many of the bodies of the deceased firefighters were never found.

We attended a funeral for a FDNY captain named Patrick Brown, the most decorated firefighter in New York. The funeral was held at Saint Patrick's Cathedral in Manhattan. The mayor and the cardinal were there. A New York cop sang "Ave Maria." There wasn't a dry eye in the cathedral. It was amazing. At that moment, I thought I must be at the most civilized place in the world.

The cardinal told a story that on the very last day of the very last Crusade, the Polish army defeated the Muslim army. That day was September 11 or 9/11. I wish that in the weeks following 9/11 the media would have done a story of it.

At nighttime, firefighters lined the streets of Manhattan. Fashionable clothes were not the uniform of the day. Blue jeans and collared fire department sweatshirts were. It was a mecca for firefighters. We were everywhere, thousands of us. The only way you could tell who was who was by reading the name of the city on the front of the sweatshirts. Boston, Los Angeles, Cleveland, Dallas, Detroit—name the city and they were there.

The New Yorkers treated us like royalty. "Keep your money in your pocket, we got it" was what you heard everywhere you went. Somehow we managed to hook up with a vice president of an international bank and her assistant. They got a limousine and took us barhopping in Manhattan in a style we surely weren't accustomed to.

The Trade Center itself was all blocked off. The only way in was with an official escort. A New York cop was escorting me there. As we were walking down the street toward the Trade Center, well-dressed people were stopping us every ten feet and saying things like "We love you guys" or "Thank you for everything" or "You're the greatest!"

It's funny, but years later, as I write these lines, many American cities, including Detroit, are facing bankruptcy. Some may end up in bankruptcy courts in New York on those very same streets that we walked along in September 2001. I wonder if any of the people that were thanking us that day are the same ones now trying to take away our pensions.

The New York cop looked at me and said, "I'll be so glad when this thing is over and everyone gets back to hating my guts."

I laughed, but I understood.

CHAPTER 36

Engine 10 is located on West Grand Boulevard, a once fashionable street that fell on hard time. The fire station is a two-story brick building located on a large corner lot. The guys do a nice job of keeping it landscaped and looking good. It was one of the nicest buildings on the boulevard. Our district covers the majority of Southwest Detroit, from downtown all the way along Michigan Avenue to the city limits.

One February night, we responded engine alone to a car fire on a side street just off Michigan Avenue. When we pulled up, I got bad vibes right away. A car was on fire in front of a dwelling. The dwelling was also just starting to burn. Whoever torched the car must have also torched the house.

The house porch and overhang were on fire, so we attacked them first. It hadn't taken off yet, so we assumed we could handle it alone. We didn't call for the box. We were putting out the car fire when the civilian who lived in the home came out enraged. He was angry, intoxicated, and probably armed, yelling, "I'm going to get those motherfuckers."

I looked down the street and noticed two cars approaching slowly with their lights off. They pulled over and parked, and all the doors opened simultaneously, and eight people got out. They all had on the same-style Tommy Bahama jackets. I reckoned they must be gang-bangers.

The man from the house started shouting, "Here come those motherfuckers now!"

The scene was starting to turn ugly. I didn't want us to be caught in some cross fire, but we were committed. We had our line and tools off the rig and couldn't just withdraw. I called Central for the police, and surprisingly, in less than a minute, a police car pulled up.

The cops got out of their car, a male and a female, and they looked like two young kids who had just come back from some suburban prom.

"What's the matter, Captain?" the female police officer asked.

I told them what was going on, and I said that I thought they were gang-bangers. "Wow, gang-bangers!" the cops said and started to laugh.

Then they immediately took charge of the scene, dividing the gang and the irate civilian up, looking for weapons, and getting everyone to calm down. Seasoned pros could not have controlled the situation better. By now our fire was out, so we didn't stick around. We put our gear back on the rig and headed back to quarters, surprised at how brave those two young cops were.

A couple days later, I was watching the evening news. To my horror, I learned that they had both been shot and killed. They had pulled over a guy for some minor offense, and he jumped out of the car with a 9 mm pistol and killed them both. They never had a chance. We rode by the scene and saw all the blood. It was sickening.

I went to the funeral and spoke to the young man's father. I told him about my chance meeting with his son and how brave and capable he was. The father thanked me. The young woman's funeral was held up north. It was another sad Detroit story.

It was okay being a captain at Engine 10. We had a great crew, pleasant quarters, and plenty of fires, although the fires were starting to get old, just like me. I started acting as chief more and more, and soon I was rarely at Engine 10. I was always on the road as acting chief.

A captain is in charge of one fire station. A chief is in charge of a group of fire stations, usually five. When the chief is off, they take the captain with the most seniority and make him chief for the day.

I came in one morning hoping to stay at Engine 10, and the phone rang. It was the senior chief, and he informed me that I would be acting chief 1 today. "Are you sure?" I asked because today was the day that the baseball all-star game was being held downtown at Comerica Park. If I was to be chief 1, an acting chief, not a regular chief, I would be in charge of the downtown area where the all-star game was being played. I was very surprised.

The Major League All-Star Game was held in Detroit on July 12, 2005. This was a huge event for Detroit. The Tigers had just built a new stadium called Comerica Park. It is located right in the middle of Downtown Detroit, which the City was desperately trying to rebuild.

Since 9/11 happened, everything was different. America was in Homeland Security frenzy, and the all-star game is one of America's biggest events. There would be no bigger event going on today in America, so it would be a prime target for a terrorist.

The feds had been in town for over a year, coordinating all the security. The department had been having meetings and training seminars dealing with today's big event, and I hadn't been to one of them. The department even sent a group to last year's all-star game to view their operations. I'll bet that none of them were battalion chiefs.

Who went? I don't know, but I could make a pretty good guess. All I knew was that today I was chief 1 (the top battalion chief) and today was the all-star game. When I arrived at the chief 1's quarters, I asked the chief who I was relieving if there were any instructions or information about the all-star game. He handed me a binder from the Department of Homeland Security.

"Everything that you need to know is in that binder. Good luck," he said.

And he took off for home. That's the way things are done in Detroit.

I leafed through the binder. Then I took a ride around the stadium to familiarize myself with it and to learn where all our equipment was placed. The department had placed a few extra rigs in service around the stadium that would be dedicated to the event. They were not to respond to anything else.

Later, when the game started, I headed over to the stadium. How exciting it was to be there at an all-star game, and being a baseball fan, I believed that I would have a chance to really see an all-star game.

They have to let the fire chief in. I was wrong. The guards at the gate wouldn't let me in. I called for their supervisor, and he wouldn't let me in either. I couldn't believe it. I was the Detroit fire chief in charge, and they wouldn't let me in the gate.

"You must have a security pass to get in. We gave the department a ton of passes, and if they didn't give you one, I can't help," he said.

"What if there is a fire?" I asked.

"Then we will let you in," he said.

"But how can you? I still won't have a pass."

He just gave me a confused look. I couldn't blame him. It wasn't his fault. He was just doing his job, and like he said, they gave the department a ton of passes. That's the way our department works—ton of passes but not one for the on-duty battalion chief. How could they always get away with this crap?

Detroit's well-known for violence and mayhem and fires. I'm sure many of the fans and media in town were looking for some of that stuff to report on, and we didn't disappoint them. Right during the game, just a few blocks north of the stadium, I caught a second-alarm fire.

We had a ten-unit row house, and five of them were burning. I called for second alarm right away and went to work. The guys did a tremendous job at stopping the fire at five units. It was the only fire I ever had that was covered by the Goodyear Blimp. Newsmen from around the world left the stadium to see a legendary Detroit fire.

I noticed that one of our union officials had shown up and was causing some kind of a squabble. I was too busy to pay attention, but after the fire was out, a local news reporter approached me and asked my opinion about the quarrel that the union official had just had.

"I don't know anything about it. I was busy fighting the fire," I told her.

"Well," she said, "the union official was arguing with your commissioner, who was here on the scene, that there was a fire engine parked at a fire station just a few blocks away that didn't respond to this fire because of the all-star game."

"That's what that argument was all about? That fire engine did just what it was supposed to do. It is here just for the all-star game. We have people from all over the world sitting in that stadium. This could be a prime target for some terrorist, and we have to have some trucks dedicated just to this event. What if there was a terrorist attack?

Wouldn't it be clever of the terrorist to set a fire and have all the equipment respond, leaving the stadium without any fire protection?"

"Yeah, that makes sense," she said.

I thought that was the end of that story, but again I was wrong. The union official who started it kept pushing the issue. The media picked up on the story, and then our commissioner made a spectacle of himself.

He held a press conference saying that he was going to find out who gave the order not letting that engine respond to fires other than the all-star game. He held his press conference, the way so many people who think they're powerful do, surrounded by his associates. The local press had a field day with this.

"If you didn't give the order, then who did? Aren't you the one in charge? What kind of department are you running?" they asked.

I'll bet the reporter I talked to at the scene was in that crowd of reporters thinking, why don't you just say what that chief at the scene said instead of sounding so ridiculous.

CHAPTER 37

2005

On the eleventh day of the eleventh month, 2005, Veterans Day, riding the big rigs ended. I was promoted to battalion chief. The red fire trucks were replaced with a red SUV with Chief written on the side. My first assignment as a battalion chief was swing chief, swinging between the Fifth Battalion and the Seventh Battalion. Both are located in Southwest Detroit. After a few months, I got my own battalion and was sent out to the Fourth Battalion, located in northwest Detroit.

I planned to run out there only until the Seventh or the Fifth Battalions opened up, and then I would head back home. When the Seventh Battalion finally opened and I was planning my return, a funny thing happened. The guys in the Fourth Battalion, mainly Engine 59's quarters, where the chief runs, asked me to stay.

It was not very often that I got asked to stay anywhere. I thought about it for a couple days, and then I decided that I would stay out in the Fourth. The other battalion chiefs thought I was foolish not to go back to Southwest Detroit, but in the end, it worked out fine.

Chief 4's quarters is a one-story building attached to Engine 59. At the back they built a newer area to house Squad 1. It is in the exact center of the Fourth Battalion with two fire stations east and two more fire stations to the west, five in all. My area of command would be from Wyoming west to Five Points and from the Jeffries Freeway north to Eight Mile, about twenty-four square miles.

Battalion chiefs only respond to box alarms and to special runs. Every night after midnight I would get at least two box-alarm fires, one going east and one going west. I would get my first nightly fire and then lie in bed, eyes wide open, waiting for my next one. Every night it was always the same. No sleep for the wicked.

The crew at 59, in gratitude for me staying, helped me fix up the quarters. It was a real dump when I first got there after years and years of neglect. We threw out all the old junk then painted and carpeted it. We then decorated the place with new window blinds and pictures. Lastly, we purchased a new TV and an apartment fridge. When finished, it was like living at the Ritz.

When they built the new squad quarters, they put in a natural gas generator. It was a beauty, a state-of-the-art V-8-powered generator that would be able to run the whole complex whenever we lost power, which was pretty often. Only trouble was that they never hooked the generator up. This really aggravated me. Whenever we lost power, we would end up sitting in the dark with no computers or base radios. All the while, a brand-new $30,000 generator was sitting there, collecting rust, for around five years now.

Getting that generator to work became a mission of mine. I found the name of the construction company that built the addition. They expressed to me that the specs called for another gas line to be supplied by the city just to run the generator. The day the City ran that gas line, they would send out a crew to hook the generator up.

I contacted the commissioner's office and was told they didn't have the money to run the gas line. They spent around $30,000 for the generator but couldn't come up with $1,200 for the gas line.

I stayed on this issue like a pit bull, writing letters and making phone calls, all to no benefit. I even had the media come out and do a story on a day that we lost power. They put the story on the five o'clock news. I was sure I would at least get in trouble. It didn't matter. The city just didn't care. When I left three years later, unfortunately, that generator still wasn't working.

We had an air-compressor station at our quarters. Most chiefs' quarters did. Unlike our generator, this thing worked. You can't fight fires without air. But it was always breaking down. Lucky for us, we had a maintenance contract with the company, so it was always getting repaired.

One day, the repairman was out fixing our air station, and I asked him if anything could be done so it didn't break down as often.

"No," he said, "we have air stations all over the world. This one and the air station on the east side are the two most overused air stations in the world. When you have that many fires and you use that much air, these compressors are going to break down. Lucky you guys have a maintenance contract."

"Yes, lucky indeed."

One sunny afternoon, I was responding to a box alarm out on Six Mile. I looked up and could see the thick, black smoke, and I knew that we had a good one. Engine 54, the first arriving engine, radioed in and said that they had arrived on the scene and that the fire was in Redford Township, a border suburb, and that the Redford Fire Department was on the scene and stretching.

We all radioed Central and went back into service, ready for another run. I decided to continue on and watch how they fight fires in Redford. Then Central radioed and said that Redford was asking for assistance from Detroit. We sent them Engine 54, Ladder 26, Squad 5, and me, Chief 4.

When I pulled up, they had a laundry mat that encompassed two storefronts going pretty good. Engine 54 and another engine from Redford both had stretched and were about to enter the building. The Redford chief on the scene turned out to be an old college friend of mine.

You didn't get many opportunities to compare your department with another department. In comparing the two departments fighting the fire, I saw a big difference. We fight so many fires in Detroit that Detroit firefighters know exactly what to do as soon as they arrive. There is no need to give them a bunch of orders.

The Redford firefighters, like most suburbs, waited for orders from their chief. They stood with tools in hand, ready to work, until they were told a job to do. There was an unbroken hose bundle lying in the street and two Redford firefighters standing next to it.

"Open that bundle, charge the line, and follow that other line in through the front door," I said.

They eagerly did just what I told them to do, dragged the line inside, and fought the fire. Afterward, Tiny Tim, a Detroit firefighter, stepped out of the fire just as they were calling for another pike pole inside. A Redford firefighter standing there with a pike pole, instead of going in himself, handed it to Tiny, who turned around and went back inside. I just figured that the Redford guy was a little intimidated.

We laughed about that for weeks, but in all fairness, it's hard to compare other departments with Detroit. Redford has a first-rate fire department, but nobody has the experience or fights the amount of fires that Detroit does. It makes a chief's job a lot easier.

CHAPTER 38

2006

"No police available," these are words every Detroit battalion chief knows. I wonder if there is any other city in America where fire chiefs hear those words. Probably not. It's no secret that Detroit is one of the most dangerous cities in America, and when we call for the cops, lots of times there are none available.

Whenever we were fighting fires and civilians threatened or even attacked us, we were stuck. We couldn't just drop everything and leave. We had limited options. We called Central for police protection, and then we waited with our fingers crossed. Whenever Central didn't respond quickly with "Chief 4, we have a scout car responding," we knew we were in trouble.

Then after a long couple of minutes, Central would call with "Chief 4, we have no police available!"

Great, we're on our own. In the couple of minutes we waited for Central for that "No police available" response, Central was frantically trying to get a cop car to respond, but none were available. If they couldn't find one for the fire department, it must have been impossible for civilians to get one. That's life in Detroit, America's most dangerous city.

At all working fires, we called for a rapid intervention team or RIT. The RIT was an additional fire company that would not go to work on the fire. They would stand by, ready to rescue, in case of a structure collapse or any other bad incident at the fire. They would usually stand off to the side with the RIT tools, out of everyone's way. When I was chief 4, I would have them stand right next to me the entire time just as additional protection from an attack by any irate civilians. A chief has to do what a chief has to do, survival in the D.

One of the worst fires I ever went to as chief 4 or as any other chief was the Pierson Street fire. It was on December 7, 2006, Pearl Harbor Day, my son's birthday. I was sound asleep. At around 2:00 a.m., Central called and woke me up and said, "Chief, you're due on a second alarm at Pierson and Tireman."

Pierson and Tireman, I thought, what could cause a second-alarm fire there? I knew the area well; it was where I grew up. There was nothing there but small bungalows. Then I remembered that big, newer apartment building they had built around thirty years ago. Thirty years old is considered new for Detroit. I jumped in my car and headed for the location.

When I pulled up, I said to myself, "Yep, that's it." It was a block-long, four-story apartment building facing Rouge Park named Parkside Manor. I parked my car on Tireman right by a hydrant with an Out of Service tag on it. I put my gear on and jogged the half block up to the fire. It was a madhouse when I got there.

There was a curved drive in front of the apartment, creating a grassy island with a fire hydrant on each end. Engine 55 was hooked up to the hydrant on the north end, and they had lines stretched into the building. I could see through the glass stairway that they had lines on all three floors. The north section of the building looked like it was going from the top floor to the bottom floor, and the wind was howling from the north. This would not be a good night.

The parking lot was in the rear of the building, and what seemed to be hundreds of people were trying to get their cars out. The narrow one-lane street in front was blocked with fire trucks trying to come in and civilian cars trying to leave. Nobody was giving way. The early winter ground was soft and mushy and, therefore, would not support any weight. Nobody could pull off the road to let a fire truck pass. It was pandemonium.

The soft, mushy ground on the front island also would not support the weight of our trucks, so we wouldn't be able to set up aerial water towers on the north end of the apartment building. It was bedlam and getting worse by the second. Chief 2 had set up command in front, and he asked me to take the back side.

I jogged to the south end of the complex to see if we could bring in any rigs from the south. I curved around the bend and ran smack into a hostile mob. Some of them were trying to exit in their vehicles, and others looked like they had just rushed out of the building. They were furious and looking for someone to blame, and here I was, a lone chief a half a block away from his troops.

"Get in there and put out that fire, you chickenshit firefighter!" one person from the crowd, who appeared to be the leader, yelled.

Then he ran up to me and knocked me down. The whole crowd started cheering him on. I jumped up and radioed for the police, and just then, two guys in plain clothes ran up and said that they were the police. I also noticed a Dearborn Heights police car parked on the corner. The crowd got worse and started attacking the cops, who said "You're on your own, Chief!" and ran off. The Dearborn Heights cop threw his car in reverse and hit the gas. It was the only time in my life that I ever saw police run away. I knew that I was in trouble.

By now the fire was starting to come through the roof, and the north wind was blowing embers down on us. It looked like a scene from the Bible with hellfire raining down on me and the mob. I was on my own and started running north toward the firefighters with the angry mob in hot pursuit. I dodged between the exiting cars finally and got to the surprised firefighters. When the crowd saw the firemen, they stopped and turned around, and I was safe. Man, that was frightening.

In that short, crazy time, the fire had advanced halfway across the building, and it wasn't going to stop there. We ordered everyone out of the building, and then, what always happened, they started radioing us back, saying, "Chief, we got it."

This always happened. The firefighters inside on the lines attacking the fire thought they could put the fire out. When we told them to get out, they radioed back, telling us, "We got it." They usually had no idea how big it was until they got out and saw it for themselves.

"No, you don't got it. Get the hell out of there!" I responded.

People often ask me if it was hard sending firemen into burning buildings. No, it wasn't hard to send them in, but it was hard getting them out. Luckily, we got them all out safely, and when they got out, they saw an out-of-control fire that was getting worse by the minute.

Because of the bad hydrants on Tireman Street, we were forced to stretch lines through the backyards of homes adjoining the parking lot to hydrants located on Braile Street.

We set up water towers on the north end, right where the mob attacked me. In one hour, the fire had progressed from one end of the building all the way across to the other end, a block-long building with all four floors going throughout. Flames were shooting into the sky, and embers were raining down. In less than three hours, the entire apartment building was just smoldering rubble.

I hadn't seen a building get destroyed that quickly since 9/11, the World Trade Center attack. The building might not have had firestops. I didn't know. But I did know this: the newer constructed buildings burned way quicker and hotter than the old ones did. An old brick or limestone apartment this size could have had fifty fires and still be standing.

Three hours after the first alarm, we were starting to pick up lines and take towers down. Over one hundred families were now homeless. Many of them were still trying to get their cars out of the parking lot. That's all most of them had left in the world. Only one person was killed, thank God. He was buried somewhere in the rubble. I don't know if they ever did find him.

CHAPTER 39

In February 2006, the city of Detroit hosted Super Bowl XL, one of the greatest sporting events in the world. Since 9/11, at big events like the Super Bowl, the feds show up to oversee security, but the fire department still has responsibilities.

The commissioner was right on the ball with this one, holding weekly meetings at fire headquarters. All the battalion chiefs were required to attend. I was surprised at the crowd who attended these meetings; most were in uniform. There were chiefs and commanders from various departments and divisions of the fire department, many I had never seen or heard of before. They were all there, taking notes, preparing for various tasks, just enjoying the moment.

I knew from past experience that they wanted very little input from the battalion chiefs. After all, what did we know? We were just a bunch of screw-offs who somehow put out all the fires and made this department what it was.

I figured out where all those Super Bowl passes would go and where the all-star game passes went. I wouldn't be surprised if some of their friends got passes.

The feds wanted us to put a fire engine inside the stadium manned with four men. The commissioner wanted to put some type of screen in front of them to prevent them from watching the game. It sounded real petty to me, but I knew it wouldn't happen because they would never figure out how to do it, so no sense in arguing.

A funny problem arose just two days before the big game. The Rolling Stones were performing the halftime show. Their stage would be a great big tongue that would be filled with wild dancing fans. The Stones would jump out of the big tongue and do their act. They had to get the stage onto the field, let the Stones perform their act, and get the stage off the field in less than thirty minutes. They found out that the crew who was going to push out the big tongue didn't have security clearances. They called and asked us for firefighters to push the stage out because we all had security clearances. We had plenty of volunteers. It was not a bad deal, get into the game for a little while and get paid too.

The chief of department asked me, "Dombrowski, do you want to be chief 1 on the day of the Super Bowl?"

"No, I got the day off and have plans, but thanks anyway," I said. He seemed surprised.

But I did have plans—to sit home and watch the game on TV. If I worked, I knew that I never would have gotten into the game. I would have been freezing my butt off a block away in some makeshift command post. No thanks. The Stealers defeated the Seahawks, 21–10.

When I became the most senior battalion chief, they transferred me to be chief 1 and sent me downtown. I didn't mind the transfer; I am a big fan of downtown, warts and all. Most chiefs didn't like running downtown because of dealing with the folks at headquarters. I made the best of it.

There is a lot more to do downtown than out in the battalions, a lot more places where a chief could hide between fires. I found all of them. I snuck in to Tigers games, Red Wings games, and Wayne State football games. On Saturday mornings, I would go shopping at Eastern Market. On nice summer days, you couldn't beat Belle Isle, our riverfront island park. I was always in the district, radio in hand, waiting for the next run.

One winter afternoon, I got a run to Belle Isle. A car had apparently driven into the river. When I arrived on the scene, there was a fire-engine crew standing on the icy riverbank, using pike poles to reach into the river, trying in vain to locate the vehicle. There was also a US Coast Guard crew standing by, observing the firefighters.

Apparently, a man driving an SUV had driven it straight into the river. An elderly gentleman standing in the crowd of bystanders said he saw the whole incident.

"The car drove straight into the water, and then the car floated out for fifty feet before it sunk. It looked like a suicide," he said.

I went up to the coast guard petty officer and asked, "Do you fellows have a boat that we could use?"

"Nope," he said.

"Do you guys have an available dive team?"

"Nope," he also said.

That's just great, I thought. It was winter, and our fireboat was out of service. The police boats were shut down for the winter too. I called central office.

"Central, we need a boat and a dive team." Good luck finding a boat and a dive team in the middle of winter, I thought.

Central called back and said, "Chief, we have DPD dive team responding with a one-hour ETA. We also have the OPP [Ontario Provincial Police] responding with a boat."

But isn't that fitting? I thought. The Canadians are sending us a boat because nobody on our side of the river has one. This was just after that jet crashed and landed in New York City on the East River, also in the winter, and we watched all those boats come to their rescue. Good luck if an airplane lands in the Detroit River in winter.

The coast guard petty officer came up to me and asked, "Did you get a dive team and a boat?"

"Yes, the Canadians are sending over a boat, and the Detroit Police Dive Team is coming. They have a one-hour ETA."

"One-hour ETA?" he said. "What do they have to do, sober them up?"

"Look here, pal," I pointed my finger and said, "if you ever make a remark like that again about our police department, you and I and your commanding officer are going to have a talk!"

What a punk that petty officer was, I thought.

A few minutes later, the Canadians arrived in a small barge-type vessel. We pointed out where the car went in, and they soon located it, marking it with a buoy.

The police dive team arrived in their box van. They were off duty and responded from home. Four of them jumped out of the van. They looked more like a grunge band than cops, and they suited up and jumped in the water. The Canadians positioned their vessel downriver in case a cop's safety line broke off and he needed rescue.

It was freezing cold, and the wind was blowing twenty miles an hour. The river, because of the six-mile-an-hour current, hadn't froze over yet. But the banks were all ice. You had to admire the courage of the cops as they dove in the unforgiving dark water. I looked over at my coast guard friend. He wasn't saying anything now.

They found the car and tied a line to it. Then they used the line to pull a cable from a waiting tow truck. In minutes, they had the car out on shore with the dead driver still behind the wheel. Poor guy, I thought. I wonder if he had a change of heart as his car slowly sunk into the river.

Because Detroit is a border city, we often had combined training with the Canadians. Underneath the Detroit River, connecting Detroit and Windsor, are two tunnels, one for cars and one for trains. The train tunnel is owned and controlled by the Canadian National Railroad.

Both ends of the train tunnel are open and unguarded, although there are security cameras on both ends and throughout the tunnel. The video screens are located in a control center on the Windsor side of the river. About twenty-six trains went through the tunnel each day.

On this particular day, the department sent a group of us to Windsor for combined-tunnel-operations school. The big reason they had the school was that Detroit firefighters had just had an incident at the tunnel and they screwed it up.

A couple months before, smoke was coming out of the tunnel, and someone called it in as a fire. When Detroit fire got on the scene and they saw the smoke, they called for the hazmat team. When the hazmat team got on the scene, they loaded up their pickup truck with air bottles and drove right into the tunnel, looking for the source of the smoke.

This is the way we do things in Detroit. We charge right in. You shouldn't do this in a train tunnel, especially if you have no idea if a train is coming. There was no fire, just condensed steam. But what Detroit did that day went viral throughout Canada. So the Canadian

National Railroad and the Windsor Fire Department decided to team up with us for some badly needed railroad-tunnel school.

They said, "Firefighters are not to enter the train tunnel until the Canadians arrive on the scene. We have all the controls and communications with the trains on our side of the river. We will respond over the Ambassador Bridge, and you must wait and take no action until we arrive on the scene." Now this is a tough one for any Detroit firefighter. They don't wait for anyone, and so came the questions.

"What if there is a fire?" one Detroit firefighter asked.

"Great question. Don't go in until we get there!" they said.

"What if there are people trapped?"

"Another great question. Don't go in until we get there."

"What if it's a hazmat situation?"

"Another great question. Don't go in until we get there."

This line of questions went on forever, and the answers were always the same. "Don't go in until we get there," the Canadians kept repeating. It was a good school, but I have to wonder, the next time there is a fire run to the train tunnel, what are the odds the boys will wait outside for the Canadians?

CHAPTER 40

High-rise fires—few things are worse for a firefighter than an occupied high-rise fire. Most firefighters in America will never see one in their entire career. My first month as chief 1, I had three high-rise fires, all occupied.

One of the first things I worried about was jumpers—the people hanging out the windows and getting ready to jump. The building was on fire, and their apartment was filling up with smoke. They couldn't breathe. Panic set in. Then they went to the windows, opened them, and climbed out. If they saw one person jump, they would all start to jump—right to their deaths. Sometimes people will do things like throw out a mattress to soften their fall. And it can be dangerous for firefighters. We have had firefighters killed by jumpers landing on them.

The next problem that I had to worry about was getting water. Like most fires, you need water to put them out. In high-rises it can be difficult. The firefighters go into the building, go up to the floor just below the fire floor, and hook up to the standpipe, the water pipes in the building that supply firemen with water. They turn it on, and after their hoses fill with water, they proceed up to the fire floor to fight the fire. As said before, when they turn the standpipe on and no water comes out, there were problems. Now those problems become the chief's problems.

One time at three in the morning, I pulled up to an eighteen-story high-rise fire, and I had both problems. The fire was on the sixth floor, and the squad crew had just radioed me that the standpipe was dry; there was no water. I had an engine hooked up to the standpipe connection out front and played away, but still there was no water. Sometimes people open the standpipe valves maliciously. When they're opened on lower floors, that's where the water goes. You have to send guys down to those lower floors to shut off the standpipes before you get any water up to your floor. It all takes time.

Meanwhile, on the side of the building, the windows were starting to fill up with people yelling for help, potential jumpers.

"Hold on. Don't jump. We're on the way," I yelled.

Just then, someone threw a mattress down. The situation was getting worse by the second.

Ladder 20 was parked right in front of the building, just like they were supposed to be, but the crew was gone. They all went in the building to assist with rescue. Except for two FEOs, I was all alone. I called for a second alarm with an extra truck. Central had sent an extra truck on the original box alarm, and thankfully, it was just pulling up.

There was a fenced-in lot on the side of the building with a locked gate.

"Bust that damn fence down, put the stick up, and start getting people out of those windows!" I shouted.

Luckily, the fire was on the sixth floor, and we would be able to reach them and the immediate floors above, but that was as far as our ladders would reach.

The water hadn't gotten to the sixth floor standpipe yet, so guys started throwing ropes down from lower floors for us to tie handlines to. Then they would stretch them up to the sixth floor. I was helping with this as I saw the first of my second alarm vehicles arriving. It was the senior chief.

The senior jumped out of his car, ran up to me, and to my surprise, yelled, "Why don't you have your fire gear on? This is a second alarm!" With all the problems the senior faced at this very moment, he chose to focus on whether or not a battalion chief was properly dressed for the occasion. I knew at that moment that I would never be like this guy.

But being the obedient chief that I was, I ran to my vehicle and put my gear on. We got water, put the fire out, and rescued all the potential jumpers. Nobody died; it was another great job by the Detroit Fire Department. I wasn't that upset over the senior's actions because I knew that soon he would be retiring and be replaced by a different senior chief—me.

CHAPTER 41

2008

My last two years with the department were spent downtown at headquarters as the senior chief. The senior chief is the third-highest-ranking uniform member of the department. The chief of department is highest with five gold stripes on his coat sleeve. The deputy chief is second highest with four gold stripes. The senior has three stripes. Both the chief of department and the deputy are appointed by the commissioner.

At the time, the senior chief wasn't appointed by anyone. He just rose up the ranks through the seniority system. After I retired, the senior chief became an appointed position. There are two senior chiefs, one for each unit. I often think that a better name for the senior would be the duty chief or the unit chief because we work a twenty-four-hour shift, and we are responsible for all that goes on in those twenty-four hours. There were one thousand men on the department in firefighting division, so divide that by two, and each senior was responsible for five hundred men.

The senior's office is on the third floor of headquarters, the most active room in the entire building. The senior's crew consists of a captain who works a five-day, forty-hour shift and a sergeant who is sent there for the first six hours of his twenty-four-hour shift. He then spends the remaining eighteen hours fighting fires back at his company. The captain is necessary to maintain the day-to-day continuity and many times is the only one who knows what's going on.

Because the senior works a twenty-four-hour shift, he has to have a place to sleep at night, and the city provides him the worst quarters possible. In the senior's office, behind a row of cabinets, they shoved in a bed, and that's the senior chief's quarters. They do have nice and quiet bedrooms down on the second floor. One used to be assigned to the senior, but now they are used as offices for all the various colleagues that the department has hired.

My first day as senior, I was welcomed unofficially to headquarters by the commissioner. He came running into the senior's office, hollering for something called the top report. I had no idea what he was talking about. There are numerous reports all over the place, and I surely hadn't learned where or what they all were yet. So as I rummaged for his report, he tossed his hands up and said, "What's wrong with this picture?"

"What's wrong with this picture!" I scornfully said. The whole office, the captain, sergeant, and the secretaries, froze and looked at me with big, wide eyes. Then the captain jumped up and handed the commissioner his report. He grabbed it and walked out. As usual, I made a good first impression.

The senior is responsible for balancing the manpower, which is harder than it sounds. We have to get 260 firefighters, all of different ranks and job classifications on duty for twenty-four hours. He is also responsible for any unusual events that take place, which there are a lot of, and any fires that are second alarm or larger.

Detroit has around five thousand working fires a year; of which, around forty go second alarm or larger. A battalion chief hates to call for second alarm. They want to handle the fire without help from downtown. They call for second alarm as a last resort. It is not unusual to have a box alarm, a one-alarm fire, with eight or nine fire companies. That is almost forty guys on the scene and still no second alarm.

I soon found out that the biggest part of my job was protecting the men, not so much at fires—the battalion chiefs did that—but in many other ways. Fighting fires is a tough job in a very tough City with tough guys sometimes doing crazy things. If the senior doesn't have their back, then who does?

One day, a firefighter on duty who feared his wife was having an affair busted out of the engine house and drove to his suburban home to investigate. When he got there, he found out that he was right, finding them together. He flipped out and beat the crap out of the guy. He then jumped in his car and raced back to the City.

His wife, meanwhile, called the local suburban cops, who stopped him at the city border and arrested him for assault and battery. He was on duty and in uniform, so they took him off to jail. We did so much to soften his charges that I thought I was going to be the one losing my job.

A fire station needed a new screen door. The old one was broke, and the flies were coming in. Who knew when the city would come around with a new one? They took matters into their own hands. They went to an abandoned home in their district and grabbed one. Now, the homeowner who lived across the street had been complaining to the cops about people stripping vacant homes in his neighborhood. The police told him next time to videotape them in the act.

When he showed the video to the cops with all the home strippers on it, they weren't very engrossed until the part when the firemen came. Firemen were stripping vacant homes. It became a big story on the local news: the firemen were the bad guys. The City wanted to fire the whole crew. You can imagine how bad we felt at the senior's office, seeing members fired for taking an old screen door from a vacant home that would soon be torched.

Firemen know that when things are going well, everybody, the media and the citizens, loves us. But when things go bad, how quick they can all turn against us.

One evening, the Michigan State Police called my office and told me they had arrested three Detroit firefighters in Monroe, just above the Ohio border. I had to go there and get their badges.

When I got there, the trooper told me that the firefighters were speeding down I-75, and he pulled them over. When he walked up to the vehicle, he said he smelled marijuana, and after he got them out of the vehicle, he found three guns. All three of the weapons were registered, and all three firefighters had CCWs, permits to carry weapons, but they failed to mention to the trooper that they had them, which is a violation of the law. He also found a bag of weed under a seat. They told him they were on their way to Atlanta for a few days' vacation.

I asked the trooper how fast they were going, and he said, "Seventy-five miles an hour." Seventy-five miles an hour, I thought. Everybody drives seventy-five down this freeway, including the semi-trucks. The police impounded their brand-new car.

They brought all three out of their holding cell and lined them up in front of the height wall.

"Sorry, Chief," they said as they saw me standing there. Then the troopers released them to my charge, and we all headed back to Detroit.

All three firefighters were black, and the police that arrested them were white. As I was driving them back, I asked them if they thought they were pulled over for a DWB, which means driving while being black.

"No, Chief, it was fair. We were going five over."

I don't think that I would have been so understanding. Cops usually give us a break for minor infractions like five over.

Then one of them said, "You know, Chief, they took my brand-new car. They took my badge. They took my gun. They even took my bag of weed. They took everything."

The next day, I was home, talking to my wife about it, and she said, "What were they doing with guns?"

"Everybody in Detroit carries a gun," I told her.

"Well, what were they doing with marijuana?"

"For Christ's sake, Linda, they were going on vacation!"

We both laughed.

CHAPTER 42

November 15, 2008, was a tragic day for the department. It was the day a firefighter named Walter Harris was killed. They were fighting a fire in an attic of a vacant building, and the roof collapsed. Walt was killed, and two others were injured.

It happened around five in the morning. I was senior chief and was awakened by a call from central office.

"Chief, we just had three firefighters injured in an east-side house fire. EMS radioed us that one of them, Walter Harris, looks very bad and could be a fatal. They're transporting all three to Receiving Hospital."

"Thanks, I'm on it!" I said.

There is no guide book up here for what you are supposed to do when a situation like this arises. I called Chief 6, who luckily was in quarters, and I told him what happened, and then I said, "You have to go get his wife and kids right now and bring them to Receiving!"

"How am I going to find them at five in the morning?" he asked.

"You have a roster of the whole battalion. You're just going to have to find them and get them to Detroit Receiving straightaway, lights and sirens both ways!"

I jumped into my car and headed to Receiving. At first, because I had just awoken, I was having trouble remembering who Walt was, and then I remembered. Yes, when I ran at Engine 23, he was on the other unit. He was a big, friendly guy who everybody liked. Walt often cooked. He made an excellent pasta salad, which he knew I loved. Walt would often tell me in the morning when I came in, "Captain, there's some pasta salad left in the fridge." It's things like that which make you remember people.

I ran into Receiving and saw his whole crew standing around, depressed. A doctor stopped me and asked me who I was. When I told him, he brought me into a side room. "It saddens me to inform you that Walter Harris has just died," he said. I left and told his crew. They were badly shaken and grabbed on to each other.

Since I was not part of their crew, I could offer nothing more to these poor guys. I walked outside and sat alone on the curb. The deputy pulled up with Walt's whole family, and I watched as they all rushed in.

Next, a familiar-looking black Crown Vic pulled up, and the commissioner jumped out. Instead of going inside, he walked up to me, pointing his finger, then angrily asked, "What happened?"

"I don't know," I said.

"How come you don't know?"

"Because I'm the senior chief. That was the chief 1's fire."

"Where's Chief 1?" he yelled.

"I don't know."

After that exchange, I left and headed back to fire headquarters. There were a hundred things that I had to do this morning, and if I was lucky, I might remember ten of them. My relief was there, and we went over the day's events.

Heading home that morning, for some reason, I decided to take a ride through a neighborhood in Central Detroit that we call the Cass Corridor. As I was driving by a bar, I noticed the parking lot full of cars with Maltese cross stickers on their back windows. I parked my car and went in.

The place was packed. I recognized most of the guys from the First Battalion.

"You guys all here because of Walt?" I asked.

"Actually, we had this planned out, Chief," a lieutenant told me. "One of the guys from Ladder 20 who's in the army reserves has been activated and is leaving for Iraq tomorrow, but it sure is too bad about Walter Harris."

I bought a round, and we gave a sad toast to Walt and a hopeful toast to the young firefighter heading off to war. Not many places other than Detroit where you would find an early morning farewell gathering like this. It's a dangerous world we live in.

CHAPTER 43

The deputy chief and I went to central office for an exercise on dirty bombs. The exercise was being conducted by a couple of army officers. I always liked working with officers rather than noncoms; they are a little easier going and more congenial than enlisted men, just the opposite of what you would think.

We were given a dirty-bomb event and then were asked how we would handle it, what our response would be. We were at the part of our hazmat team showing up with their radiation detectors, and the colonel stopped me and asked, "You guys have that stuff?"

"Sure we do," I told him.

"Is there any way that you can get your hazmat team here and we could take a look at their stuff?"

"Absolutely," I said, and I called central office and asked them to send us the hazmat team.

"I'm not sure that we can do that," the deputy said.

"We can do anything. You're the deputy," I lightheartedly responded.

When our hazmat team showed, I was surprised and embarrassed to learn that we didn't have the equipment that I told the army we had.

"No, this is good for us to find out," the colonel said. "We want to know exactly what you have and don't have. The first twenty-four hours of a disaster, you first responders are on your own, and then the federal government shows up with everything you'll ever need."

That's comforting to know, I thought.

"Where would you put all your equipment?" I then asked.

"We find a vacant big-box store in the area, and we use that."

"What if there is no vacant big-box store in the area?" I asked.

"That's impossible. There is no area in America that doesn't have a vacant big-box store close-by."

"That is an amazing fact," I said. "But it's nice to know that you guys got our back as far as what we need. This is Detroit, and we will need it all!"

The first lady, Michelle Obama, was coming to Detroit. The Secret Service called and said her plane would be landing at Detroit City Airport at 2:00 p.m., about three hours from when they called.

"Guess what," the captain said, "the airport rig is out of service."

"Wow, the first lady's jet will be landing at an airport with no crash crew on duty!"

Then the Chief of Department came running in, shouting, "Oh my god, Michelle Obama is landing at two o'clock, and the airport crash crew is out of service!"

It was moments like that that made my job so interesting. Because of low manpower, we usually took the airport rig out of service and sent the crew to help man an engine company. Now we we're screwed if anything happened to that plane and no crash crew responded. The entire third floor would be hung from a tree. And you can't send just any firefighter there. They must be certified by the Federal Aviation Administration, the FAA.

Well, in the end, it all worked out like it usually does. Larry found us a crew and took an engine out of service to man the airport rig. When the first lady's plane landed, the airport crew was ready and in service. Someday, unless they change the way they do things in Detroit, they won't be that lucky.

Another big difference from working in the fire stations as opposed to headquarters was the romance. The fire stations were 95 percent men, and the closest thing we had to romance was a locker full of old *Playboys*. But at headquarters, it's different. There were a lot of women, who were mostly secretaries, and men, who were mostly chiefs and department heads. Romance, it seemed, was in the air. It usually followed three steps.

Step 1, two people start flirting with each other. Step 2, there are rumors of a secret relationship. Step 3, charges are filed for sexual harassment. Then come the usual restraining and police-protection orders, and various people aren't allowed to go into some areas or offices at headquarters. It was a way of life down there.

Devil's Night is always an interesting night for Detroit firefighters, and my last one on the job was memorable, but not for the best reasons. Everybody on the third floor works Devil's Night, and like everyone else, I spent the night running all over the City.

I was at a second alarm on the lower east side. Someone had lit an old factory on fire. It was out, and we were picking up line. The guys had been working pretty hard and were exhausted as they picked up the line.

I walked around the corner, and there was a dozen of our new soon-to-be firefighters. The training academy had a class, the last one for many years to come, and the instructors brought them out this Devil's Night to help out. At the moment that I walked up to them, they were sitting around chitchatting, taking a break, I presumed.

"Hey, guys, they need a hand picking up line around the corner," I told them.

They all got up and started to walk over when one of them said, "They got enough people over there." And a few of them sat back down.

"You don't give orders around here!" I said. "Now get up and get over there. That's an order."

They all got up and went, except for the one trial man, the one with the mouth. He slowly shuffled over while giving me this it-isn't-over look! I couldn't believe this was who the city was hiring. This group wasn't like the usual group of new firefighters, who were usually young and eager and hoping to make a career as a Detroit firefighter.

Instead of hiring a group like that, they decided to let people from other departments transfer over to the fire department. We got a group of mostly middle-aged folks, some with attitudes, who knew better than letting some chief give them some shit. I wonder how many of these guys will still be on the job in five years and not be sitting at home with a taxpayer-funded duty disability?

I really hated to leave this great department that I loved so much, thinking that this was the type of people who would be taking our places. There is nothing more important to this fire department and to this City, I would argue, than to hire the best people you can, young, healthy, eager, respectful men and women who will proudly serve this City for the next twenty-five, thirty, or maybe even thirty-eight years!

CHAPTER 44

2010

June 7, 2010, was my last workday. My official retirement day was June 26, exactly thirty-eight years from my first day on the job, but June 7 would be my last. I was leaving a little early. Most retiring firefighters work right to their last day, and I wanted my friends to think that I would too. I just wanted to leave the way I came in, without any fanfare—not that I expected any.

I controlled the chief's schedule, and I marked all my remaining workdays with sick days and an unused furlough. That was my secret. But it didn't last long. I was in the office, and an east-side battalion chief named Tim was looking at the chief's schedule and said, "Hey, Bob, this is your last day!"

I tried to deny it, but he knew better.

"What are you going to do today, your last day?" he asked.

"Nothing, I'm just going to hang out here and have a quiet and peaceful last day."

It turned out to be a nice day. There were no big fires, no major problems, and nobody punched anyone. The chief of department and the commissioner (a new one, who I liked) couldn't have been nicer. I bought little gifts for the secretaries, and I took the crew who worked in the senior's office to lunch.

Five o'clock rolled in, and everyone left for home, and I had the whole place to myself. Then the phone started ringing. A few different engine houses must have heard it was my last day and invited me for chow. I thanked them all for their kind consideration, but I figured that I would just stay put.

Then I got a call from a sergeant who invited me to Engine 46, an east-side engine house.

"Thanks, but I'm just going to stay here."

"Baloney," he said. "This is your last day. You can't stay there all night. Just stop by for five minutes. Your buddy Chief 9 is here waiting for you!"

"All right, I'll stop by for five minutes."

When I got there, I was surprised to see that practically the whole east side was there, some of the guys I didn't even know, but they were all great, offering their best wishes. Every on-duty battalion chief also managed to stop by. Roscoe, the funniest person on the fire department, maybe on the planet, sang me his version of "Happy Trails to You!"

It was a great last night, and I was really glad that I went. I even managed to cover up a minor fender bender that someone had. What more could a senior chief ask for on his last day? I thanked them all and headed back to headquarters for my last night.

I woke up early and cleaned out my locker so that I could leave as soon as I was relieved, no tearful good-byes. I loaded up all my stuff into my brand-new Cadillac, which was parked on the first-floor apparatus room.

I had bought my Cadillac just for this occasion. I never had a nice car like that before. When I was a young man on the job, a retiring chief came to work on his last day in a brand-new Cadillac. He said to me, "Kid, after all these years, I've earned it!"

I agreed and told myself that when my day came, I would do the same thing. I was just glad they still made them.

I was back up in my office, waiting for the OFU, other fuckin' unit, to show up when the department radio sprang to life. The familiar, pleasant voice of central office said, "It's 0630 hours. All companies resume your wakeful watch. Congratulations to Senior Chief Dombrowski on his retirement after thirty-eight years of faithful service to the city of Detroit!"

I sat there, listening, as calls of congratulations were radioed in from all over the City. As this was going, the other unit filed in. I silently sneaked downstairs, hopped in the Cadillac, put in a Van Morrison CD, and headed for home.

People have often asked me if it was hard to leave after all those years, and I had to admit that, yes, it was kind of hard to leave, especially for those first two blocks. Then I crossed Third Street, hit the gas, and it was easy from there.

EPILOGUE

On July 18, 2013, my sixty-third birthday, the city of Detroit declared bankruptcy. Actually, the state of Michigan declared bankruptcy for them. Michigan governor Rick Snyder and his handpicked henchman, Kevyn Orr, a bankruptcy attorney from Washington, DC, decided after an exhausting three-month investigation that Detroit could no longer function. It had to go bankrupt. Oh, and happy birthday, Bob Dombrowski.

The announcement was made on the afternoon news. It was carried live by most of the local stations. It was a strange scene. The two of them dressed alike in dark suits and red ties, looking into the cameras with their best we-tried-everything looks, and blamed, among other things, this bankruptcy on us retirees and our outrageous pensions. The reporters in the crowd loved every minute of it.

The governor stated that he only has the best intentions for this godforsaken, union-loving, welfare-collecting enclave, which gave him less than 10 percent of the vote in the last election.

"It takes fifty-eight minutes to get a police car to arrive, and that's just wrong," said our governor.

At that moment, I thought some reporter would have raised his hand and said something like "Well, Governor, you've been in office over two years now, and what have you done to help Detroit other than to cut state funds?"

But no such luck; the show went on for what seemed to be half of the afternoon. When it ended, the media made them into a couple of Joan of Arcs coming to save our corrupted town.

The active firefighters fared no better. Snyder and Orr want to get rid of our beloved seniority system so they can promote who they want. What that has to do with Detroit's finances, nobody knows. But there is nothing the union can do about it because Orr threw out all the contracts. He could do this because of a bankruptcy law that the politicians just passed in Lansing similar to the one that the voters voted down the previous November.

They also want to take away the active members' pensions and free health care and then make them do first-responder runs like they do in the suburbs. Orr says that he's not planning to cut their pay anymore, and he really can't. Detroit's pay has been cut to the bone. A new cop or firefighter starts at around twelve dollars an hour. That's along with paying for a big part of their health care and a 401(k) instead of a pension. Not too rewarding for serving in the most dangerous city in America.

Our pension is 96 percent funded, and it is backed by the constitution of the state of Michigan. But Orr and the governor tell us that it is not protected when we get into federal bankruptcy court. Federal law trumps state law, and our protections could be gone. This same prediction is echoed daily in the Detroit media and by every good citizen at all the local coffee shops.

I wonder just what we did to deserve all this anger. I went to work every day for thirty-eight years, and every time the bell rang, I jumped on the rig and did my job. People always came up and said how much they appreciated the job we did and how difficult it must be. Now some of those same folks are rooting for us to lose everything we worked for. The average Detroit police and fire pension is around thirty thousand a year, and we do not get social security. A firefighter or police officer retiring today with thirty years on the job gets around forty-five thousand a year, again no social security.

One writer in the local media even said not to feel sorry for us because some of us are living in homes in Livonia. Yes, that's right, Livonia, Michigan, where the average median house value is around $145,000. I guess he feels we have no right to be able to live that well even after thirty-five years of fighting fires or crime in Detroit. Perhaps we should spend our retirement years living under an overpass, going to the back door of some rectory, and begging for a bowl of soup.

I can't completely blame the way my fellow Metro Detroiters act. This area has been so beaten down and so many people have lost their jobs and homes and their self-respect that they have nothing left but anger and hate and resentment. And all this is being easily exploited by an overzealous Snyder and Orr.

Kevyn Orr has hired appraisers to see what he can get for the art in the art museum, which is figured to be billions. He's planning to sell off the parking meters, the streetlights, the buses, the water department, and Belle Isle, our famous island park. They even sold Detroit Fire Headquarters, the five-story Albert Kahn–designed building right in the heart of Downtown for a measly $1.25 million. He's getting rid of 150 years of a proud history all to save the city, he says.

And now, the Red Wings are getting around $400 million in bonds for a new arena right in the middle of Detroit's bankruptcy. Orr hired a new police chief for $140,000 a year but bumped it up to $224,000. He gave his buddy Brown, a council member who supported him, the same $224,000, a nice raise from the $85,000 he was receiving. He also sends his old law firm in Washington, DC, $1.3 million a month faithfully. And we thought those crooked Detroit mayors threw taxpayers money away.

But he is being frugal with some expenses. He stopped paying most of the city's bills, including the millions that they owe the pension fund. And he's not even paying his own rent. Kevyn Orr is the man they sent to straighten us out, the man who had his own home back east foreclosed and who is living in luxury at the Westin Book Cadillac Detroit Hotel rent-free. When asked by the local news who is picking up the tab, he looked into the camera with his big toothy grin and said, "I don't know."

As I write this, some of the media is starting to turn on Mr. Orr. The *New York Times* says Kevyn Orr is in the bankers' pocket in their report "No Banker Left Behind." An article in *Bloomberg News* says

Kevyn Orr's plan to pay the bankers 75 percent and the retirees 20 percent is a perversity. But best of all, Michigan's own attorney general, Bill Schuette, broke with Orr and the governor and stated that, yes, the constitution of the state of Michigan protects our pensions.

At these trying times, I sit back and think how trivial all my previous complaints about the department were. How hard it must be for all the great men and women still on the job, who are now worrying about their own pensions, their medical insurance, their working conditions, and even their jobs. When I retired, we had a minimum of 260 men on duty. Today, that number is 140. How low morale must be. But they are still fighting the great fight, trying to keep the fire department that I loved together. Good luck and hang in there Detroit's bravest.

About the Author

Bob Dombrowski was born and raised in Detroit, Michigan.

The author is a retired firefighter from the city of Detroit, and is hoping he doesn't lose his pension. He is happily married to his wife, Linda, and has been for over thirty-five years. They have three sons, Andy, Bobby, and Kevin.

He is a boater, who is desperately trying to sell his boat. He is passionate about the sports teams out of Detroit, his bike, his dog, his before-dinner-cocktails, and enjoys a good political debate.